SILENT CRY

Echoes of Young Zimbabwe Voices

SILENT CRY

Echoes of Young Zimbabwe Voices

'amaBooks

BRITISH COUNCIL | 75 YEARS OF CULTURAL RELATIONS

ISBN 978-0-7974-3821-7
EAN 9780797438217

Published by 'amaBooks
P.O. Box AC1066, Ascot, Bulawayo
email: amabooksbyo@gmail.com
www.amabooksbyo.com

Project facilitated by Butholezwe K. Nyathi

Project funded by British Council

Cover artwork: Gilmore T. Moyo

Cover design: Veena Bhana

This book is a work of fiction: any characters, organisations and
situations mentioned bear no relation to any real person, organisation or
actual happening.

Contents

Part Two: Silent Cry

Introduction

Butholezwe K. Nyathi

We are delighted as the British Council Echoes of Young Voices youth group to be involved in this publication of a collection of short stories and poems by young people from Zimbabwe's second city Bulawayo. This book combines the pieces in English from the two publications in Zimbabwe, *Echoes of Young Voices: Identity and Diversity Beyond Scribbled Words*, which was nominated for a Zimbabwe National Arts Merit Award, and *Silent Cry: Echoes of Young Voices II.*

Echoes of Young Voices is part of the British Council's international Identity and Diversity project, which aims, using the arts, to encourage young people to challenge and address stereotypes, prejudice and negative perceptions in order to develop mutual understanding between young people.

Literature is a powerful medium of communication. It enables the reader to view the world from the perspective of others. Literature can invoke different emotions in the reader, of joy, of fear, of sadness, of empathy. It allows the imagination to run wild. Creative writing particularly engages the mind; it is the product of a fertile imagination and encourages free thought and expression.

There is a need for literature by young people for young people. There have been few opportunities for up-and-coming young writers to be published in Zimbabwe and even fewer for their voices to be heard outside of the country. The book enables the young writers to tell their stories, stories that have meaning for them, stories that should be read and enjoyed by young and old alike.

I, on behalf of the Echoes of Young Voices youth group, would like to thank British Council Zimbabwe for their support of the project, all those who helped in the publication of the book, and all those young writers who submitted stories and poems for consideration.

Glossary

Al-salãmu alaykum – peace be upon you
Amangqina – cow hooves
Amahewu – traditional beer
Baba – father
Burg – town/city
Ekhaya – rural home
Enkomponi – compound, the ghetto
Hijab – the headscarf worn by many women in Islamic countries
Ingagara – people of higher status
Ingwebu – opaque beer
Iwe musikana, wuya pano – hey young girl, come here
Izinyoka – snakes
Lobolo – bride price
Mafikizolo – Johnny-come-lately, newcomer
Malokozana: daughter-in-law
Malume – uncle
Mealie-meal – ground maize
Mfana – boy
Mkhweyana – son-in-law
M'zambiya – wrap of material from Zambia
Muti – medicine
Omalayitsha – cross border transporters
Omatshay'inyoka – unemployed people who hang around street corners
            (literally, people who beat snakes)
Sadza – mealie-meal porridge
Salalas – people of high social class, who are presumed to eat salads
Samp – chopped maize
Sekuru – uncle
Umgaxa – lazy dog
Umkhemeswane – a local fruit
Ungabi le pressure – don't worry
Uyahlanya kanti – are you crazy
Uyangikhafulela – you are spitting on me
Wena – you
Windie – commuter omnibus conductor
Xahu-xahu – a local fruit

Part One:

Identity and Diversity
Beyond Scribbled Words

Just Trust Me

Bongani Ncube

I am a street kid. Don't ask me why I speak the Queen's language better than the Queen herself, just trust me: I am a street kid.

I've seen broomsticks thicker than my arms and the look from my eyes calls for the invention of a new word. The sight of my dirty face has cracked many mirrors and even more hearts. I am a street kid.

But don't pity me, it's all good. I mean, I am freer than most of you; no restrictions, no parents to hassle me, I can do whatever I want. No school, no work, no obligations, no strings attached. I can roam the world whenever I choose, wherever I choose, with whoever I choose, as I choose.

I am a nomad in a desert. Only I know where the best food is to be found, where the best takings are to be had. Only I can make a living from the streets everyone else just passes by. At night, when the rest of the world has retreated in fear to the safety of their homes, only I have the courage to continue prowling.

This is the life! It's life on a permanent holiday. I sleep anywhere as long as my body fits. I've become adaptable, evolved into a new and higher species: homo sapiens urbanus.

In the morning, woken up by the first rays of the sun caressing my face, I scrounge around for food. Bakeries, restaurants and shops throw out as much food through the back door as they sell through the front. But don't tell anyone, that's our little secret.

From then on, it's anything I want. A spot of begging, a sniff of glue, or a round of 'borrowing' items from shops and flea-markets. I think you might call it shoplifting, but that's such an ugly word.

And I am a beautiful person. Underneath all this dirt and grime, this tough talk and vulgarity, there is a really beautiful person. It's just that sometimes he's buried so deeply, even I can't find him. But that's the thing to remember, there is a beautiful person... I hope.

Who am I trying to kid? If I was such a beautiful person, would my mother have dumped me as a baby? Wouldn't she have nursed me and held my hand when street urchins like me stared enviously at us? Where is she now? Am I that ugly?

Am I that unfortunate, condemned for the rest of my life to sleep under stormy skies and blazing suns? Did I say the sun caresses my face? Oh please, it slaps me senseless. Adaptable my foot, concrete is concrete and whichever way you look at it newspapers aren't really cut out for a career in acting – they make lousy blankets.

Sometimes it's too hot, sometimes it's too cold. Sometimes people notice me, most often I might not exist for all they care. I don't know who I am. I'm so sad, there's a blank space in my heart.

According to the United Nations, there are almost a million blank hearts in this country. Blank hearts that have had to watch their friends jailed, watch others die of AIDS. Blank hearts with no identity. Their suffering is played out like the deathly notes of a violin – 'Somebody help me'.

The state bought four hundred million dollars worth of new weapons. They might as well shoot me first – only a few dollars would buy me a square meal. Otherwise everyday the violins keep on playing, and I listen, along with a million others, waiting for my violin to play the last notes and announce my ultimate glory – death.

I apologise. I lied to you in the beginning. I who can count my IQ on one hand, who am I to mislead an intelligent reader such as yourself? The truth is, my short life is agony. It has been since I was born, the birth pangs of my mother echoing throughout the rest of my existence.

I am a street kid. I suppose that's just the way it is. Don't ask me why. Just trust me.

My Tribe

Bubelo Thabela Mlilo

Am I Shona?
My mother's grandfather was Shona
But he grew up in Matabeleland
And married an Ndebele woman.

Then am I an Ndebele?
Maybe.
My mother's father grew up
as an Ndebele but he
married a Sotho woman.
So perhaps I am Sotho.

No I can't be, because my
mother was brought up as
an Ndebele.
But then again am I Xhosa?

My father's mother was Xhosa
and her father came from
South Africa a long time
ago. Mtotobi Mlilo also came
from South Africa long back.

My father was brought up as an
Ndebele, so that makes me an
Ndebele.
But my mother's family calls my
father a Kalanga because he
comes from Kezi.

So what am I really?
I think I should be
simply called a
Zimbabwean.

Scattered Hearts

Novuyo Rosa Tshuma

The first thing that Nqabutho saw when the door hurtled open was the ugly head of his father's knobkerrie. It had a deep crack in it, permanently crooked into a malicious smile, as though relishing the task to which it had been assigned.

He winced - he could never rid himself of the memories of that knobkerrie and the damage it had done to his buttocks as a child. The old man came charging into the room behind the knobkerrie, his sagging belly swaying wildly from side to side as he swore through short, furious breaths. He skidded to a halt by the sofa on which Nqabutho sat and swung the knobkerrie savagely at his son's temple.

Nqabutho ducked in terror into the arms of the young man seated next to him. The club whooshed past his right ear and thudded into the sofa. His mother's delayed shrieks stabbed the air as she stood helplessly by the door behind her husband, clutching the colourful doek that decorated her head. But John D. Nleya was deaf to any pleas. He took another swipe at the two young men clinging to each other, they dived to the floor, and once again the helpless sofa took the punishment. Swearing profusely, the old man loomed over the two, his rage refuelling. That his own son, a man, should insult him and his ancestors by daring to bring into his home this…this… accursed thing that was squirming beneath him, was an absolute abomination.

Spurred on by the ferocious roar of its master, the knobkerrie again swiped through the air. Screams erupted from Nqabutho who only stopped yelling when he realized that he did not feel any pain. It was then that he looked into the face of Batsi beneath him, and saw that a black bruise had

5

been depressed on it by the fist of the knobkerrie. With an irate cry, the boy attacked his father, forcing him down onto the sofa in his attempt to throttle him. For a moment the elder man could not comprehend what had just happened, so shocked was he that his son would dare to pounce on him like that. This time, Mrs Nleya was bold enough to take action.

"Heh, Nqabutho, have you gone mad! Let your father go, let him go!" The robust woman enveloped her son in her huge arms and dragged him to the floor. It took a while for the old man to get up and retrieve his weapon. The next moment, he was looming over his son, poking his face with the butt of his club.

"I do not have a son who is a woman, do you hear me!"

"I am not a woman," Nqabutho intoned, each word pronounced slowly and precisely, as though explaining a difficult concept to a child.

"I do not have a son who loves another man as he should a woman."

Nqabutho shut his eyes for a moment, trying to quell the flames that now threatened to overwhelm him.

The old man dashed to the television set, pointing at the grey screen. "Is it this ugly box, eh, this ugly, stupid, talking machine?"

Without waiting for an answer, he heaved the television set with all his might and it crashed to the floor.

"Baba, baba, please I am begging, stop!" But Mrs Nleya might as well have been talking to a deaf man.

John D. Nleya leapt to the little radio, smashing its front. "Is it this singing box, eh, that fills your mind with rubbish, eh? This brainless thing that causes your ancestors grief in this way?"

The crash of the radio as it hit the floor was the only answer the old man wanted. He swung his club at the dusty set of wine glasses on the cupboard shelf, at the china, a gift from Mrs Nleya's mother, at the family portrait housed in a ceramic frame, at the twirling, crystal swans that Mrs Nleya had bought before her son had been born, at his own favourite mug that he used to drink *amahewu* and displayed proudly to his friends, at Nqa's twenty-first birthday key made of glass. All these items that had built the cupboard into a monument of family history and beauty crashed to the floor, and lay broken and spent, forming a shimmering carpet of broken glass and ceramic, the perfect mirror of the scattered hearts that thudded painfully in the sitting room.

Silence, save for Nleya's heavy panting. Then Mrs Nleya's stifled sobs.

The old man stared at his son, the son stared back. Nleya's eyes refused to acknowledge the boy lying next to his son, writhing in pain. It served him right, Nleya thought. He was glad to have inflicted the pain. Surely it was incomparable to the deep hurt that surged through him at that moment. It was numbing enough to have to think of the kind of serious help that Nqabutho needed. One could not just play with the ancestors like that. He had seen a boy once, a little younger than Nqabutho, back in his rural home, who had suffered the same affliction. His family did everything they could to convince him to stop his cursed ways before it was too late. But the stupid fool would not listen. Even one of the elders warned him, but a fool does not always know that he is a fool. Within three days of the warning, poof! The boy fell sick. He could not remember to what false malady the hospital had attributed his death, but it did not matter. Everyone knew the true cause of his death - one simply did not play with the ancestors.

Slowly, the old man nodded, his sagging jowls dancing rhythmically. "Tomorrow, you and me, we are going *ekhaya*. Tomorrow. You have insulted the ancestors. They must be appeased."

But the boy shook his head firmly. "No, I don't care about the ancestors. What I care about is... is us, my family..." he paused, "and Batsi."

Nleya trembled visibly. "Tomorrow, we go. The elders will know what to do. Whatever has possessed you can be removed from your being."

It was then that Nqabutho decided to let the hammer fall. "Batsi... Batsi and I are getting married in South Africa. We are allowed to get married there."

His father's features were twisted by rage once more and Nqabutho was afraid that he would attack them again but he didn't. Nleya simply stood cemented to the floor, staring at his son, his only son, his only child.

"And who will be the *malokozana*, eh?" he demanded, his voice coated with contempt. "Who will be the *mkhwenyana*? Who will pay *lobola*? Who will be the head of the household? Who will bear the children, eh, Who! Who!"

"We are getting married, and we would be happy if you could be there to share our joy."

The old man's body tensed. How could he make this stupid boy realise the absurdity of what he was saying? It simply could never work; African culture could not allow it. Instead, he, Nqabutho, and the rest of the family, would be a laughing stock. The shame of the city.

"Look," he said to his wife. "Look at your son. Is this what you taught him?"

7

Mrs Nleya turned to her son, tears still pouring from her puffy red eyes. "Please Nqa, please, this is a sin. You are offending God's Holy Spirit …"

"Just shut up! Shut your mouth! Now I see. This is all your fault! All along I have tried to be the true black man, committed to his roots, while you poison my son with that white man's rubbish! God this, God that, God what!"

Silence. Then Nqabutho's voice sailing softly through the air. "Don't blame yourselves. I don't want you to do that. This is simply how I am. It's just difficult to explain. You see when I look at Batsi… I … we … I just love him…" He stopped. He stopped because his father's eyes were brimming with tears. In all his twenty three years he had never seen his father cry. The old man let go of his knobkerrie. It landed on the floor with a dull thud, and rolled aimlessly for some distance, now totally powerless, harmless. A tear spilled from his left eye. Pursing his lips, he turned away from his son, and dragged his feet across the glass-littered floor, oblivious to the pain as the shards stabbed his flesh. The fury was gone, the rage had evaporated. In its place was shame, shame that his seed had produced such a social misfit. He disappeared through the door.

Nqabutho swallowed hard. He wanted to cry. He was tempted to deny his feelings, but remembering the past strengthened his resolve. He remembered the unease he had felt in the company of girls, not the giddy excitement that his friends professed to feel. He remembered the fear and the confusion. What if his father's ancestors paid him a visit, perhaps cut off a limb, or if his mother's God sent a never ending storm of hell fire to scorch him. And yes, he had been ashamed at first, but he wondered, did anybody understand what it was like to live a lie? He had not deliberately chosen this. It was him. This was what made him happy and being with Batsi brought him real joy.

A year ago he had been banished by his parents when they discovered that he was gay. He had returned to try to gain acceptance back into his family, to make his parents understand him and in the end he had made his father cry. Guilt rapped at the doors of his heart.

When he first arrived, alone, a few hours earlier, his parents had hailed his return, berating him for having been silent for so long. His mother's eyes had lit up as she gushed over him and ushered him into the same old sitting room. The surroundings were the same but he had been taken aback by how old both his parents now looked and he had prayed that he was not the accelerator of their fast forward ageing. His chest still ached from the smothering hug his father had actually managed to give him. It had been in his eyes, the hunger he had harboured for so long for his son.

He realised that they had taken his return as a sign that he was 'normal' again. Seeing his father engulfed by so much joy at his presence had almost encouraged him to retreat to the pit of cowardice, until the arrival of Batsi.

Batsi's family had not jumped with joy at the revelation by their son that he was gay, and the ensuing introduction of his life long partner, another man, but at least they had not shunned him. Their unconditional love was guaranteed. How naïve he had been to believe that his family would accept himself and Batsi into their home in the same way. Had he forgotten his father, the staunch traditionalist and his ancestors? Or his mother, the rigid Christian who stuck solidly to her dogmatic principles, except, of course, where her fearsome husband was concerned? He had wanted his family back, as simple as that. And all he had succeeded in doing was making his father cry.

His mother's sharp voice jolted him back to the present. "… two men at the altar is not a wedding! It's an insult in the eyes of God! For one man to love another is a sin. Read Leviticus 18 verse 22…"

Nqabutho sighed. "Mother, please."

She began sobbing again. "It's hard enough to accept that you are … that you are not normal! All right, I will accept it, but will you stop this crazy idea of a wedding?"

She looked so desperate that he was tempted to give in, but one look at Batsi and his heart began thundering in his chest. In that moment, he knew without a doubt that this was his partner for life.

"It's not a church wedding, mother. We just want to make it official, like other people. This is your gay son, mother, and this gay son would be the happiest man on earth if you attended his wedding."

This only made her cry harder. "Your father is right, I failed you as a mother! Oh God, what didn't I do! I committed him to you, did I not? I took him to church whenever I could, did I not? I taught him how to pray! … Nqabutho, what you need is prayer!"

He remained calm. "I don't need prayer. What I need is for you and father to accept me as I am and love me. None of this is your fault. In fact, it's not a fault, mother. Just allow me to be happy please."

"Even at the cost of your family? Two men, getting married? It's against tradition. It's against God. You are offending the Lord! - All right, do what you must, but please, do it in private. Why must you rub it in the face of your

9

family, shaming us all like this?"

"Mother, stop."

Her hand grabbed his frantically. "Listen, I know many beautiful girls around here, I will introduce you to some today ..."

"Mother!"

"No, Nqa, no! A wedding between two men. How can I rejoice in that? There is nothing to rejoice. It's tragedy."

Nqabutho sighed heavily. He had tried. He had failed. He gazed at Batsi, who nodded imperceptibly. It was time to leave.

Batsi held out his hand. Nqabutho clasped it, and gently pulled the love of his life to his feet. He looked around his family home, and his heart bled. The shards of glass pricked his heart; the violence of which the sitting room reeked saddened him, for he had been its instigator. He did not know if he would be back. Without looking at his mother, he picked up the single suitcase and gently propelled Batsi to the door. When he opened it, the sun sailed through, and a river of warmth meandered through him.

"Nqabutho!"

His mother's voice, right behind him. He stopped. Her hand shoved a bulky wad of notes over his shoulder.

"I hope this will help," she said

He opened his mouth to stammer a protest, but she cut him off swiftly.

"No. I want you to have it. Just some savings I have been keeping."

Emotion welled up in him. He turned and gazed at her for a long time. His mother. He had to see her again, someday.

She smiled. "I am your mother, and I will always love you. See this?"

She patted her round belly. "Nine months you were in here. I felt pains to get you out!" She laughed. "Heh, you were a big one," her eyes scoffed. "You suckled milk from my breast. A father can denounce his child, a mother, never!"

He bent down and enveloped her in his long arms. "Goodbye, mother."

She wanted to shake him then, to make him change his mind, to make him see that this evil boy next to him, this lost soul, could never supply him with love that could compete with that of the Almighty. He could not see, he just could not see that, by his actions, he was crucifying her heart, driving the nails of pain and shame deep into her soul. She wanted to shake him, to slap him, to plead with him once more to abandon the deadly road on which he was treading. Anything that could make him change his mind.

Instead, she managed a rueful smile. "Goodbye."

He turned around, one arm gripping Batsi, the other their suitcase, and they slowly trudged across the dry earth to the rusty gate.

Outside, dirt covered children were furiously chasing a plastic ball, and shrieking in delight. Across the dusty road, Nqabutho could see one of his mother's friends, MaSibanda, busy pegging clothes, her back to him. His eyes drank in the scene before him greedily, the children, the little houses huddled together, the incessant noise and chatter. A wave of nostalgia swept over him and a deep melancholy settled in his heart as he faced the prospect that he might never be welcome here again.

The Death of My Father

Mercy T. Dube

His sunken cheeks, his inward looking eyes-
The sarcastic smile on his lips, the unkempt hair-
The rough hands - all spoke eloquently of the life he had lived,
But I could not mourn for him.

He built wonderful mansions yet squatted in a mud house
And slept on a bed full of bugs.
The hammer, the saw and the plane were his tools and damnation.
I could not mourn for him.

He fashioned dining tables, chairs and wardrobes.
Sweat was his ointment and perfume.
No. I could not mourn for him.

I had already inherited his premature old-age look, imbibed
His frustration, but his dreams of happiness were my love, my song.
Yet I could not mourn for him.

He died in the green of summer yet I shed no tears.
I watched the coffin as it slowly went down.
The sound of the shovels filled my ears, my heart bled.

I remembered his sandpaper hands, his love for me
In spite of his differences with mother.
I decided to forgive him, remembering the pains he went through.

My father's dead life still lives in me,
I will awaken his sleepy hopes and yearnings.
Yes. I will mourn for him.

Jabu's Journey

Babongeni Zangelo Mlilo

It was a bright Zimbabwean morning when, the day after his mother's funeral, Jabu arrived with his mother's friends, the Ndlovus, at the bus stop in the dumps of Harare. Mr Ndlovu asked an old man if this was the bus to Bulawayo and he said yes. They jumped onto the bus and found Jabu a seat. Jabu began to cry and, on asking him why, he replied that he was scared of AIDS as it had killed both his parents. The man sitting next to him, who had been reading a newspaper, overheard the conversation and quickly changed his seat. Seeing this Jabu became more uncomfortable, despite Mrs Ndlovu's efforts to calm him. When it was time for the bus to leave the Ndlovus said goodbye and got off the bus. During the journey Jabu kept on thinking about the man who moved from his seat because of what he had heard.

Jabu arrived safely in the city of Bulawayo. He caught a kombi to Nkulumane, where, by showing his scrap of paper with the address written on it to various people on the street, he managed to find his uncle's place. After a few days his uncle started looking for a school for him. Luckily he came to ours. I noticed that Jabu was always a lonely fellow, so I asked him why and that's when he told me that his parents died of AIDS and about his experience on the bus. I felt for him because he had lost his parents and was feeling lost and thought people wouldn't like him, just like that man in the bus. My friends and I decided to make him feel welcome at the school. We had been taught in school that you couldn't get HIV from playing with somebody. Jabu and I have been friends ever since.

13

My friend Jabu made that journey when he was ten years old. Now he is twelve and has a happy life. Children who have lost their parents need love and assistance. So let us put our heads together and find ways of helping them.

R. I. P.

Lesley Phiri

Church

A man of God is heard
He is shouting, sweat on his head.
He says I am a social misfit,
I need Jesus in my life.
Simply because I'm a ragged vagabond
I am labelled the worst sinner.

Society

I inherit my grandfather's knobkerrie,
I carry it wherever I go.
People give me all sorts of names:
Prophet, Moon, Apostle step-on-the-rod...
I'm only preserving culture yet
I'm said to be worse than Lucifer
Because of a simple knobkerrie.

School

My right hand holds the Holy Bible to my chest,
My left hand raises the knobkerrie.
They say that I'm strange,
A round nut that has fallen into millet.
Life is sourer
Because of my identity.

Love

Oh yes!
She is my bread.
When I'm hungry, I love her.
My mother won't hear of her
Simply because she is older than I -
And she is HIV positive.
That does not matter to me:
Love conquers all.

Deathbed

I threw away the Holy Bible,
I'm suffering from spiritual amnesia.
I threw away the knobkerrie,
My ancestors are after my blood.
My HIV positive blood.
My mother just died of a heart attack.

Epitaph

Prejudiced against,
Stereotyped,
Denied identity.
Rise. If. Possible.

"Diversity is not an abnormality but the very reality of our planet."

Chinua Achebe

My Sisters' Clothes

Sarhanna Hassim

Sobs wrack my body. The knife hacks at my skin, guided by my hand. The poisonous blood I was cursed with has to get out of me. I stop and stare around. No noise disturbs the night, and there is no witness to this act. A cold wind blows through the barren field. Crooked trees leer at me. I carry on with the job. Finally there are enough cuts on my body to drain every drop. I lie down as my blood seeps into the earth. I am satisfied.

I think about the time when we lived in the township. My father ran a tuck-shop and had a high standing in the community. My mother would sit outside in the sun, plaiting her friends' hair and gossiping. My older sisters would huddle in groups with friends, giggling and eyeing passing boys. I would go to school and then be free to play for the rest of the day. That was our daily life.

One of my favourite activities was sneaking into my sisters' wardrobes when I was home alone. I would try on the bras they used to cover their budding breasts, slip on dresses and high heels and prance and preen in front of the mirror. My stomach would ache with excitement and I would tremble all over. I felt complete and self assured. I would then quickly strip and fold the clothes neatly so I wouldn't get caught.

I am not sure of the exact events surrounding our departure from the township. I do know my mother cried for days before my father decided we would go back to his homestead.

I was filled with mixed feelings about our new life. The smells of the homestead were overpowering. The stench of animals in their pens and human labour lingered in every corner. It was a great relief to me to find out my duty would be to take the goats grazing. The games the boys played sickened me. They constantly fought over nothing and when I would not join in they were merciless. They called me *umgaxa* and other degrading names. I started believing their words. To escape them I would go into the forest and pick *xaku-xaku* and *umkhemeswane*. Hiding there I would cut myself with an old kitchen knife I had found. I would tear at the skin of my body where nobody would see. The strange pain relieved me, but what I needed was to play the special game of the township to make me feel better and special.

One day, when I was free and everybody was on a trip to town, I sneaked into the girls' hut. There I performed the almost sacred act of dressing in their clothes. As I twirled I heard a deep voice behind me. I froze in fear as I realized Uncle Mbazo was standing behind me. The tone of his voice changed as he spoke to me. He promised not to tell anyone what he had seen if I would do him favours.

So began the most horrifying period of my life. I trembled with fear every time someone told me Uncle Mbazo was calling me. I knew that when he finished ripping into me with his male hardness I would not be able to sit for days. I stopped eating as I could not bear the thought of mixing food with what he made me swallow. My father was too drunk on *Ingwebu* to notice what was happening; my mother was too sunk in depression to care about me. My sisters rarely saw me as they worked from dawn to dusk with the older girls. Everybody else thought I was lucky to be getting so much attention from the head of the family whom they all worshipped.

I started living in a world of my own. I did not interact with anybody. Sometimes I escaped to the forest and ran, screaming for help, but nobody ever came. I woke up at night sweating, shaking, and hating the curse I was. The curse that caused my family's failure in the township. Young people kept away from me pointing out my wild eyes and sunken cheeks to each other.

I did not care about any of this. I felt a horrendous aching pain in every part of me. My soul shattered and crushed, my heart full of holes. My pain immeasurable, unbearable.

The climax to this came when Aunt Gugu found her husband corrupting my body in their hut. She flew at her husband, rolls of fat shaking and eyes rolling, pulling him off me. Aunt Gugu then turned to me, screaming as she kicked my head and body, calling me a husband stealer. With those words she destroyed every bit of male pride I had held onto. Uncle Mbazo stood immobile as his wife raged. I dragged myself up and forced my battered body out of the hut. I walked away blindly, stumbling and shuddering. Finally I lay

18

down here in this barren field.

I watch the last of life ooze out of me. Nobody can touch me now. My eyes shut and I am transported to peace and happiness.

Identity

Munyaradzi Alfonce Gova

With you

        I find reason to live

The beauty

        To discover who I am inside

The capacity

        To reflect the me in the world

In you

        Lies

My pride and power

Sistas

Babusi Nyoni

The cloth drops onto the floor and cockroaches scurry away, abandoning their futile search for food. Rainwater trickles into the bucket in the corner.

A tiny ray of light permitted by the clouds illuminates a poster that reads 'Heavenly Home', the words in contrast to the surroundings. A rat scuttles across the floor and disappears into the shadows of the sleeping section. A woman stifles her sobs and the rain does not stop.

The woman, Sandra, painfully stoops to pick up the cloth. She takes it and wipes the tears from her eyes. Slowly she moves to the place she calls a lounge. She tries to hold it in but it overwhelms her, this pain that makes itself known only through endless tears. She screams an obscenity in her mind, afraid of stirring the baby growing inside her, although she knows in her mind that she hates the baby. The baby and its father. But maybe not the baby?

"Why did it have to be another male?" she thinks, having convinced herself of the baby's gender. A girl would have made her happy. Wouldn't it?

She feels sick, unsure as to whether this is due to her physical condition or her emotional state. She lies down for a while and is on the edge of slumber when a knock on the door rattles her. It's Pretty, her close friend, who opens the zinc sheet obscuring the doorway and lets herself in to find her 'sista' curled up in a shivering ball, despite the warmth from the smouldering fire. She walks over to Sandra's side and helps her sit up. Compliant, Sandra props herself up on her friend. They are silent. Water trickles down the sides of the wall. The baby kicks softly.

It was Jerome. The name that was to come up whenever tears were in abundance. The two had met at the launch of a 'Better Schools' campaign, stealing glances at each other across the hall. Eventually she had plucked up the courage to initiate conversation with him, despite words of warning from a friend, one of those who have deserted her. Now her world has changed, friends have become foes and foes... are foes all the same.

They began to grow fond of each other. Reciting plagiarized poems and whispering their hopes and dreams. Besotted with each other, they engraved their initials, bounded by heart shapes, on tree upon tree.

How she had loved the security of his strong arms. Gone now are the days when she would rest in them. Cradled in them, daydreaming of the culmination of their relationship – their marriage. An event that would be serenaded by the liquid voice of the country's top crooner; a day where champagne would cascade from a fountain; an event the bride would wish would never end. The culmination of a relationship that Sandra now wishes had never been.

Pretty ponders as to what might be going through her friend's mind but the blank stare is difficult to interpret. She opens her mouth to say something but common sense compels her to shut it as she realises it could be another one of Sandra's bad days. Pretty hopes that her friend will not succumb to the depression that destroyed her mother.

After the wedding was called off, Sandra's mother broke down. The pain of watching the dreams she had for her daughter crumble was overwhelming. She tried to be strong at first, helping her daughter rebuild her life, but in the end the stress cost her her life. Sandra was now alone, her father had been killed just before her tenth birthday. He was mugged on his way home from his factory job, just another docket to the police.

After her mother died, she was forced out of the only home she had known by a pack of property - hungry uncles who cared nothing for their niece.

Pretty looks at Sandra, banished to this place where no man aspires to anchor. She is now a figure that no man dares afford a second glance; even a first is too much. She is nothing now.

A quilt of plastic bags shrouds the roof. Car parts and pieces of zinc sheets form her walls. She sleeps on the naked earth lulled by the pulsation of footsteps outside, always moving, tempting her to join in, and paining her for she cannot.

The virus thrives within her, like another child. A twin to the baby inside her. "It must be a male," she thinks to herself, certain that a female would never do this to another. "Why did Jerome do this to me? Why did he rape me? Why did he destroy our dreams?" she screams. Pretty is silent, she gets up to place a kettle on the fire and returns to her place beside Sandra, as if she hadn't heard a thing. She stares at the floor, wondering where MaNkomo is.

MaNkomo is the only other person unafraid enough to befriend Sandra. They had met at the social welfare offices trying to get some support, with no success. She is married to a polygamist and has mothered eight children. Pretty, on the other hand, lives with her parents and at the age of thirty-four has abandoned all prospects of marriage. That is the bond she shares with Sandra. A bond neither one of them is going to break.

On cold nights the friends sit around the fire escaping the cruelty of their worlds by imagining how things might have been. But today is a different story as the realities of this life have caught up with them.

The rain has stopped outside. Pretty sees that the water she had put on the fire is beginning to boil, so gets up to make a cup of tea for Sandra in the only cup in the household. She replaces the kettle on the smouldering embers and returns to Sandra's side to find her crying.

"Why me? Why rape me? What did I do to deserve this? Huh? Answer me!" Sandra pleads.

Pretty has no answer.

The clouds give way a little and a beam of light brightens the shack.

Pretty moves closer to her friend. "Be glad that you still have tomorrow. No-one can take that from you if you don't let them."

Sandra smiles faintly at these words as Pretty takes the cup to the fire to refill it.

Sandra muses, "Some friends are still friends." And maybe, just maybe, she'd be able to live this life. Not just survive it... .

Racial Harmony

Nadia Gori

For decades, you and I have hated each other,
For decades, you and I have been fighting,
For decades, you and I have killed
Too many innocent souls,
Agreed to disagree.

But today I am putting a stop to it.
Today I want you and I to unite,
Today I want us to pull like one team,
To work together and bring and preach
Peace amongst different races of the world.

I stand tall today because,
My brothers and sisters, racism has to be made moribund.
Racism is undesirable because it does nothing
But sow destructive seeds of hatred amongst people.
I believe the world is for all races to live in peacefully.

Let us plant seeds of love in our hearts,
Show not ignorance, but respect for each other,
For there is diversity and dignity in all races,
Which gives us the vitality of life, the beauty under our skins,
For under our skins we are all the same.

Skin

Thando Khuphe

As a child I was a very handsome boy. I still am, in fact, but not as I was during my childhood. At kindergarten people used to mistake me for a girl, but once put straight would exclaim in surprise. People assumed that I looked like my mother but quickly changed their minds once they met her. They then thought that I took after my father, only to be disappointed once again. I looked like neither of my parents nor any of my close relatives. I looked like my unique self and I was proud of that, even as a child.

Despite knowing that I was good looking, I grew up a sweet, loving, and respectful child, thanks to my mother who made sure of that. Had it not been for her, I daresay I might have taken the compliments paid to me to heart, becoming a pompous and vain misfit in society. Instead I let mother mould me into an asset to society, a pleasure to look at and delightful to know. I was not that hard to mould since I was a willing student.

My good looks only lasted until I hit adolescence, when things started happening to me. First my voice changed, then I became taller, taller than my mother. But the greatest blow of all was the attack on my handsome face. Suddenly it was like chewed bubble gum that had been rolled on sand. This was very worrisome to me and I turned to my mum for help.

"It is part of growing up son," she said calmly. "You will be looking as good as new by the time you are eighteen. These spots will become a distant memory to you."

"Eighteen?" I said incredulously. "Mama, I am only thirteen, and, while I wait to turn eighteen, are you sure there is nothing that can be done?" I went on pestering her.

"Well there is, and it all depends on you." She paused and I listened attentively. "If you keep on pestering me about something that is beyond my control you will earn yourself a smack on your behind!"

That shut me up, but it made me even more determined to find a remedy for my blighted face. The first steps in my quest were to give up sweet things like minty chocolates and to apply face creams stolen from my mother.

As I progressed further in high school, my obsession with my face did not diminish. Some people of my age had smooth unblemished skin. If having bad skin was part of growing up, were they not part of the growing scheme? I tried to talk to some of the boys who were in the same sinking boat with me. Unfortunately, they were either blind to reality, or too stupid to view the boat as a sinking one.

"There is nothing wrong with getting pimples at our age," one of the boys called John said. "It shows that we are becoming men." He paused and I looked at him quizzically.

"These pimples," he went on squashing an especially juicy one near his chin, "show that we are thinking of girls and girls' pimples show that they are thinking of us. As for you," he said, scrutinizing me, "you have an awful lot. Which girls have stolen your heart?"

I did not bother to answer and instead stalked away.

School closed for the holiday and I took the opportunity to raid all my female relatives' make-up bags, but it was all in vain. I was still as pimply as ever and, by the time school opened, I was pimplier if that was possible. Sakhile, a girl in my class, caught my attention on the very first day school opened. Her once pimply face had been transformed to become smooth and blemish less. We became good enough friends for her to share her secret and for her to bring it to school the very next day. It took me almost two weeks to realize that I was not getting the same results as her. If anything, my little friends had multiplied and became fatter and juicer.

When I turned eighteen, two things happened to me. My mother's words fell down, I lost faith in the Ndebele proverb which says 'The word of an elder does not fall down' and I fell in love. Her name was Marie Ann, a classic beauty who was later to become my wife. When I first saw her, she sat on the back seat of a kombi, features calmly composed, saying nothing, her perfect skin seeming to beckon to me to move closer. I did so and was smitten. Her skin must have been the major attraction, but, as I got to know her better, I decided that, skin or no skin, I would have fallen in love with her anyway.

My relationship with Marie would have been a bed of roses had it not been for our skin differences. My Marie had little sympathy for men who worried about the condition of their skin, let alone those who chose to take special care of it.

"That is why you have never seen face creams for men being advertised on *our* national television," she would say. "Whoever heard of men who put on make up? What would the world be coming to? And fussing about it when we are in public, I get so embarrassed. I would appreciate it if you would not mention your skin in private either, but I guess that would be asking for too much hey?"

"That's easy for you to say. If you were in my skin you ..."

"I am not, so it's no use saying ..."

"You are! You are getting under my skin."

"Oh I am sick and tired of the word skin, skin, skin, skin, skin, skin this, skin that. Don't you ever want to talk about something else beside skin?"

I caved in, and never again during our courtship mentioned the word skin. After all you win some, and you lose some. To win my Marie I had to lose some skin.

At twenty seven, I asked Marie to marry me and she obliged. I looked thirty two and she looked twenty one, although she was only a year younger than me. I wished there was someone to help me look my age. My wish came true in the form of a wedding present. The wedding present that saved my skin came in the form of an old issue of South Africa's *Men's Health*, which was addressed to me, accompanied by a letter. Since Marie and I had just become one that day I had no choice but to give her the letter to read. She promptly gave it back to me pointing out that it was after all personally addressed to me. I started reading.

Hi

Many congratulations on your marriage. Unfortunately I could not be there, but if you are reading this, it shows that you received my present. Life has been kind to me recently and I am now employed by the South African magazine Men's Health. I even have my own column in the section Sex and Relationships entitled Girl Talk.

My present to you is on page 138 in the enclosed magazine, I ...

I stopped reading, grabbed the magazine and quickly opened the page.

"December 1999? It's pretty old, what is in it anyway and who sent it to you?" Marie asked, reading the date on the cover, as I scanned page 138.

"Yeah it's old," I echoed her. "Just stuff which has nothing to do with me," I said straight faced, ashamed of myself to be already lying to her on our wedding day. "It's from a high school friend Sakhile," I added, tossing the magazine under the bed. Marie did not comment and we continued opening the other presents, but all the time I was thinking about what I had read so far.

In the early hours of the morning I crept out of bed, reached underneath it, found the magazine, then stole out of the bedroom so as not to wake Marie. The bathroom seemed the ideal place to read undisturbed. The article had been written by a Jacci Pestana and was entitled *Cracking the Moisture Myth*. Pestana had certainly done his research. The article discussed the different skin types and the moisturisers and face creams needed to maintain good looks. Especially made for men! When I finally finished reading the article over and over again I had cramp in my backside, but this did not matter because I was a changed man inside and about to change outside too, I hoped.

Marie and I have been married for almost a year now. She is pregnant with our first child and her once unblemished skin has become all pimply. My mother says that is to be expected during pregnancy and that the pimples will vanish once she has given birth. I do not believe her and I think neither does Marie, because she has been buying all kinds of creams from the pharmacy, but they do not seem to be working.

As for me, at twenty-eight I now look at least three years younger, thanks to my morning and evening rush to the garage every day. Once there I ply loose one of the boards covering the inspection pit. Beneath are an assortment of creams and moisturisers that I acquired on the advice of the magazine article. Their use has saved my skin and made me handsome once again. Marie thinks my looking good has something to do with my being married to her, but of course I know better. Maybe one day I will tell her the truth, when we have solved our skin differences.

Bones

Khumbulani Malinga

Father – the diviner,
Father – the bone thrower.
A bone made Eve,
Mbuya Nehanda's bones arose.
Father, a thrower of bones.
Bones are to him
What a bible is to a Christian.
Neighbours fear him.
Christians say: he is an occult priest.
Christians read the bible,
Father studies bones,
The spirits interpret the bible,
Ancestors reveal the mystery of the bones.
So why is father lambasted
By the holier than thou?
Marriage of the bones and the bible
Produces a ticking time bomb against the devil.
Africans –
Slumbering in identity crisis,
Embracing foreign gods
And denouncing their forefathers.
Bones.
Father – the diviner,
Father – the bone thrower.
I - the bible reader.
I - the Christian.

Being Different

Tanya Hunt

When I was ten years old, I moved with my family from Zimbabwe to England, and it was then that I became aware of just how diverse people are. The area we settled in, Gloucester, was a very pretty area, but the culture and customs differed so much from my own that I was too busy trying to fit in to even notice the scenery. Coming from Zimbabwe, with its politeness and relaxed atmosphere, I found it difficult to accustom myself to the brash and busy English lifestyle. The people I met and socialised with were often rather hostile because I was from a little known land far away, and I gradually fell deeper and deeper into the void of despair.

Due to my different nature and upbringing, I found it difficult to make many friends, and the English children did not seem very interested in forming any kind of meaningful relationship with me. I moved through my years in England as an outcast, an outsider, different from everyone else, and it was during this formative time of my life that I struggled to find my own identity.

With the crush of peer pressure, as well as other influences around me, it was very hard not to adapt. However, I rebelled against the conventional English image, and instead of trying to fit in, I refused to change to suit the preconceived ideas of others. I stuck to my opinions and stood up for myself and, through a long, tedious, emotional journey, I finally managed to win the respect of my English peers.

It was very difficult to maintain a strong image, and even harder to continue to believe in myself, and there were many times when my resolve weakened. I faltered then, but with the support of my family I managed to hold myself together. I built up a reputation of being strong and unbreakable, and able to handle anything. However, deep down inside I doubted myself, and often, when I was alone, I cried - tears that failed to bring solace. Whenever I reached this depth of desolation, I picked myself up and dried my tears. No one saw this, for I hid it well. I had to be hard. I had to be cold. I had to be uncaring. I had to be unflinching. At the first sign of weakness, I felt my peers would be prowling like hungry beasts, ready to tear me to pieces.

I wanted to be accepted and welcomed so badly that I was turning into the very person I had not wanted to be. I had become cold and unfeeling, with no kind words for anybody. I was horrified to discover that, in trying to distance myself from what I was afraid of, I had done the very thing I had set out to oppose; I had changed myself to fit in.

Once this became clear to me, I realised that I was living a lie. I was not unfeeling, I cared! I cared about everything from environmental issues to other people's feelings. Especially about other people's feelings. I had been hurt too many times by careless words not to care. When I became aware of this, that I did care, I felt as though a great weight had been lifted off my shoulders and my chest. I could breathe again. I was happy again. I had spent all this time struggling to cultivate a false identity, because I was afraid of being too different.

At the end of almost three years in England, I returned to Zimbabwe, my home. As I walked back into my old life I mused over what I had learnt from my experiences. Diversity was good, I decided, because it provided a challenge. It had prompted me to learn more about myself and in doing so discover my very own identity. I came to the conclusion that there can be no identity without diversity, for how can we attempt to be individual if we are all exactly the same?

Look At Me

Zisunko Ndlovu

Look at me,
Not for examination
Or note taking
Not for questioning
Or gossip spreading
Not for disruption
Or quake making
Not for modification
Or fabrication
Not for interrogation
Or correction
Not with a shunning gaze
Or cunning faith.

Look at me,
For hope and life
In me lies.
This, a just mind
would realise.

The Beggar

Novuyo Rosa Tshuma

She simply stood there, her huge, beautiful, brown eyes boring into mine. Snot dribbled from her nose to her dark lips, she licked it absent-mindedly. Her little cup was raised to the general public, pleading for any generous hearts. She seemed oblivious to the hand-bags that were clutched to armpits, or the cold eyes that quickly looked away from her. I think her dress had once been red. It was now faded and blanketed by blotches of grime.

Then, boldly, she approached me. From where I stood some distance away, I was attacked by the odour that clung to her. I dug my hands deep into my pockets, in search of some loose change, but she did not ask for money. "I am going to be the Vice President of Zimbabwe," she blurted out, her face lighting up as she gave me a proud, brown-toothed smile.

Her eyes reflected her experiences on the ugly side of life, whose mere contemplation would cause most to wince in pain. She turned away from me, and that was when I noticed her soiled feet. Deep gulleys raced furiously down them, the aftermath of a never ending flood of poverty. Then, the next moment, she was gone, scampering with great agility over her territory and disappearing into an alley.

I was deeply moved. There she had been, this tiny street kid with few prospects but to continue her family legacy on the grimy streets of the city, confiding her dream to me. I wondered what had inspired her to aim so high when she was so low. Could it be that by the appointment of the first female Vice President in Zimbabwe, this dirty beggar girl had been moved enough to see herself rising from the dreary pits of bleak poverty to such dizzy heights. "I am going to be the Vice President of Zimbabwe."

I sighed, remembering a world unknown to me reflected in her eyes. I hoped that she didn't become Vice President. She had enough in her heart to make it to the Presidency.

Diversity

Munyaradzi Alfonce Gova

It is a prize
A gift
And the way forward.

The Token Woman

Lindah Mafu

I emerged from the building, filled with pent-up rage. I had been locked up in it for three years. I was now twenty four years old, light in complexion, medium-sized, with blackish brownish eyes that could change colour depending on my mood. I looked back at the building. I had learnt many skills there. The first being self defence. There was no-one to defend me in there. So I learnt to give back as good as I got. Three years in Ncube and Associates was enough to drive any normal person crazy, unless that person was crazy to begin with. Like my boss.

My boss. He was slim and elastic in movement. From his looks, you would think that he was a born follower. But he was over-bearing, manipulative, arrogant and self centred. I hated him. I am not ashamed to confess that if he had been hit by a car directly in front of me, I would have definitely looked sideways and crossed the street.

I began to think back to three years ago. I could feel my face burning with embarrassment, humiliation, anger, failure and some other strange emotions that I could not lay my finger on. I could still recall, vividly, the first day I came here. I had been naïve. Being fresh from university, clutching around me a trove of dreams and hopes, I looked forward to my first job. I had been too cocooned in my world of fairytales to actually realize that, out there in the big world, lurked a monster called reality. I had stood outside this building with my impressive university passes smiling at the tremendous success I would achieve once I set foot inside it.

I soon realised that I had got the job not because I could do it, or because I was trained to do it … No! It was because of affirmative action. The company had started employing women just to convince others that it had a progressive gender policy, but they didn't. My boss could not hide his hostility towards me. The fact that most of my colleagues had the same attitude made the going tough. They made it clear that they did not believe a woman could stand in front of a judge and win a big case. So I got the bread-crumbs, that is the miserably pathetic cases that all the males refused. Over the years I watched with increasing anger as less qualified and less able people, men, rose up the ladder of promotion whilst I remained at its bottom, receiving hand-me-down cases.

I heard sexist remarks everyday as I walked into my office. Some idiots would say, '*iwe musikana, wuya pano.*' Others had the temerity to cat-call when I passed. One colleague, I remember acutely, grabbed me from behind one day. I was so angry that I made a sharp retort and slapped him. Whereas I expected an apology, he asked me what I'd expected when I came to work in a firm largely populated by men.

I tried my best to win my colleagues' approval, but to no avail. They always seemed to enjoy mocking me whenever I made the slightest mistake. My boss's hostility to me got worse as time went on. When I complained about the kind of cases I was given, he said I was still a newcomer, an amateur, so I needed to learn the rules of the game before I was assigned to the big cases.

I kept on working hard and nagging him until he finally, and very unwillingly, assigned me to help one of the senior partners, Mr Dlamini, on a very big case. I did not know what would happen if we lost, but I could guess - I would be laughed at. So I worked really hard, researching the case and studying the relevant law every day and night before the case came to court. After many gruelling days in court, we won. When I got back to the office, I hoped that my colleagues would at least give me some praise for our success. But no. Several of them commented I had helped win the case because I was a woman and the judge pitied me. I was livid. My boss' remarks were, "you sure impressed the judge, never thought a pretty thing like you would help win a big case, unless you did some favours for the judge." All this was accompanied by a suggestive leer. I had had enough. I wasted no time in telling him what I really thought of him and of the policy of luring women into the company just so they could be abused. Then I turned to my co-workers and told them what I thought of them before turning and storming out, with my chin held high. That is how I came to be standing outside the building and all it presented to me. It was a place where I had been misused, degraded and debased. I was now waiting for Monday. I had no doubts about what would happen then - I would be getting my marching orders.

Monday came. I approached my work place with mixed feelings. I would be sad to leave the place with a heavy burden of failure. At the same time I was glad that I had not allowed my workmates to simply carry on abusing me. So it was with immense trepidation that I pushed open the door. The office was quiet as I walked over to my desk. On the desk was an official looking envelope, and my heart sank. I ripped it open, to find a note from the senior partner, Mr Dlamini, praising the work I had done on our case and commenting that the company's affirmative action policy was beginning to bear fruit and that he would welcome my input as to how it could be improved.

From that day onwards, things began to change slowly for the better. I am working on more interesting cases, more women have joined the company and my colleagues have begun to recognise my value to the company. And to top it all, my boss has also had a change of heart and is considering me for promotion. I now see a future for myself and other women at Ncube and Associates.

Between the Lines

Brian Dzapasi

Nothing is ever what it seems:
The sky above may not be so blue,
You could be a figment of your dreams,
The mirror reflection might not be you,
Seemingly simple elements might as well
be complex.
And it follows that the reverse could be true,
That we are who we think we are.
But the life that we survive, the air that we breathe,
The family and friends we share,
The wisdom and wealth we acquire, with time...
Every one of these could be a decoy,
A deceptive way of concealing the real us
From our inquisitive selves.
We seek immortality, we mix potions,
Life seems too short to be real,
Immortality too far to reach,
Too unimaginable to long for.

We recollect, in a flight to the past,
A picture, which shows us who we might have been
At a certain moment within a static second:
A startled look, a matching suit, polished shoes,
And, just before the shot, a forced smile.
We are an ambiguous parable
Whose meaning seems to lie deep within us,
Yet we spend lifetimes in search of it.
And so we scratch the grave
Into a heap of our own dust.
A few might know, but they won't
Know that they know, and

In oblivion they lug their knowledge,
To the grave and, just
A moment too late, realize that they knew.
For nothing is as simple as it might look,
Neither is it as complex as it might seem.
All is deception.
We are masters and victims of this game,
For we deceive to live, and live to deceive,
Lost and found in the dimensions of time, the matrix.
Seconds, minutes, hours, days, weeks,
Months, seasons, and years are spent
In search of our identity, the hunger to know
Who and what we really are.

On the Streets

Michael Hove

To be honest, I really don't know myself, but I do know that I am a living being and that makes me subject to death. At one point I was born and at one point I will die. Mortality, that is simple biology that you and I don't want to accept. A popular writer once wrote, 'It is life when ancestors give with one hand and take away with the other.' It is life.

Right now I honestly don't feel like telling you my story, because I'm having some personal problems. Do you want to know what's bothering me? I know you do. Okay, it's my girlfriend, she just dumped me, can you believe it? She says I'm not as tough as she thought I was. Tough love, I just can't give her that. Well, not that I can't give her that, but I just don't want to. And do you know what she said? "What a dumb blond, and a coward to boot." Life has to go on, we win some, we lose some. I can't change the way I am. How can she compare me to those fat black bullies with heavy chains hanging around their necks? They just sit there at the rubbish dump by the train station. They just wait, just sit waiting. I don't know what they are waiting for. How can someone just wait, for the whole day? You need to exercise at least, no wonder they are fat. Can't they look for jobs? Well… I might forgive them on the issue of jobs. Jobs are hard to find these days, our hope right now is the next year's police intake and competition is stiff. You just have to impress them, otherwise you'll find yourself heading back to the streets fighting for food. Such is life.

I hate the environment at the train station. You see different kinds of people, each and every one of them minding their own business. Many people prefer the train because it's cheap. They call it the Freedom Train. Things are not so good these days on the economic side. Most people cannot afford to buy a packet of fresh chips these days. But a few can and, after eating, they sometimes leave one or two chips and throw the container away. With lightning speed, that fat black bully quickly pushes you aside to catch the container before it hits the bottom of the bin. Arrogantly he munches the discarded chips as he walks away. The next person comes and there is an action replay. It's not fair, this time it's a pie. I love meat pie. Imagine that juice mixing with your saliva. It is the survival of the fittest on the streets.

Sometimes it's not the local travellers giving us something to keep our stomachs quiet, it's the tourists, wandering about with their heavy baggage. They've heard about the misty waters of the Victoria Falls that flow the whole year round, as if telling the sun that it does not know its business, because the water never dries up. Even David Livingstone knew that. The most the sun can do is to blend with the mist and create a colourful rainbow. All this I've seen on paper. I've never been there myself. How can I?

The other day I went for a pee outside the train station with my friend Billy. I know we had not eaten anything for the past two days, but what Billy did shocked me. He started eating grass. Grass with chlorophyll! Grass of all the things on this planet, whether you're poverty-stricken or not, it just doesn't make sense. He's supposed to be a carnivore not a herbivore. "It's my body, I know what I'm doing," he defended himself. On our way back to the station, Billy started to vomit. I knew something bad was bound to happen. It was his body anyway. Just ahead of us two guys were talking about how badly they were treated at their workplace. They were talking about their wages. "We get peanuts. And the cost of transport. It's better not to work. I hate it. I really hate it," one of them complained. Such is life in the urban areas. Life can be so tough, especially when you are not educated.

Before I lived in these dirty streets, I received a little bit of education. My master taught me the basics, but that was not enough to help me fight this battle on these streets. After my master died, I became homeless. The fire ate him in his sleep, he had forgotten to blow out the candles. How painful. I miss him a lot and I also miss home, my ever warm carpet, it was burnt too. Right now I'm adapting to a new life. I'm learning new things, meeting new faces. As a dog, I'm prepared. Are you?

Part Two:

Silent Cry

The Controller of the Queue

Novuyo Rosa Tshuma

If you really intend to make any progress in any queue where I come from, you'd better make sure your strength and stamina are as strong as your desperation. Better be prepared to give as good as you get; even the old ladies put up a good fight I tell you. Perhaps it's only the banks that don't tolerate the nonsense of a crazy crowd stampeding through their doors, the way they always do at the supermarkets. Civility has become an outmoded concept and contending against those crazy crowds certainly calls for ruthlessness, where even your neighbour becomes your adversary.

Take my neighbourhood shop, for example. There's one incident, and one man, I will surely never forget. The man was a local resident, a gardener; I have never seen anybody put up such a performance! He had taken over as the 'controller of the queue' as soon as the *mealie-meal* truck arrived at the shop. He stood on the top step of the supermarket, with the cream-coloured grains lacing his upper lip like a neat moustache. He stood in his filthy clothes, throwing his hands about clumsily in an attempt to bully the frenzied crowd into order.

There was a queue for the men and another for the women, then a special one for the women with babies, but none for the elderly. Many were scrambling to borrow a baby for the special privilege that this bestowed.

This particular war called for stamina as elbows rammed into stomachs, bad-breathed mouths issued violent protests and young men inveigled their way towards the front of the queue. A girl in a mini skirt was standing some metres away, where the angry feet could not stir the dust onto her *Vaseline* smeared legs, a look of disdain frozen on her face as she eyed the *mealie-meal*

45

bags with feigned nonchalance.

A fight broke out between two women over a bag of *mealie-meal*. Raucous laughter erupted from a gang of youths who began to chant "*Tug of war! Tug of war!*" until with a *rrrr* the bag ripped open and the spilt grains merged with the disturbed dust and danced around the angry feet. The women lashed out at each other, squawking and clawing, until one man dragged his wife from the fight and silenced her with a slap. Meanwhile, people, like a pack of blood-maddened scavengers, scrambled for the dusty grain, scooping it up, along with the soil upon which drunkards had urinated, into cans and paper bags and anything else they could lay their hands on. The 'controller of the queue' pointed and gesticulated, throwing his limbs about like he was about to jive, until he was frothing at the corners of his mouth.

One woman made the mistake of saying, "*Baba, uyangikhafulela,* you are spitting on me."

His eyes swelled, became two moon-like orbs with the wire thin veins threaded around them. "I am spitting on you!" he exclaimed, his arms akimbo in disbelief. "Woman, I'm trying to help you and you say I am spitting on you!" he screamed. "You girl, *wena!* You say I spit on you, me!" he continued, reducing the woman to a girl. He poked his chest with his *mealie-meal* coated finger. "Do you know who I am? I can ban you from getting a bag, do you know that?"

He spun around to the crowd, picking out the women with his glare. "Did I spit on any of you?" Silence, talking eyes glancing furtively around.

His wife, with legs so long it was as though she was standing on stilts, was gazing at the ground, searching, I'm sure, for a hole in which to shovel her embarrassment.

"You girl! Do you know how many children say 'Father' to me? Yet you disrespect me! *Wena,* I will…" And he made as if to slap her. She thrust her bottom lip forward, the stumps of rust-coloured hair plaited in white thread jutting from her head like angry witnesses, protesting against these accusations.

He was in full flow now, on stage, the superstar in some great film playing itself out in his mind. Spluttering, his voice growing louder and louder. "Do you know who I am? *Do you know who I am?*"

He poked the policeman who was issuing the *mealie-meal* tickets and demanded that 'this girl' be banned from buying any. And when, a moment later, the policeman handed her a ticket, he guided her and her baby forward with a rough hand, saying, "This way, Ma, but you said I spat on you.

Anyway, give this woman a bag."

I felt ashamed for him. He continued to yap like he had to cough something out of his chest until members of the crowd yapped back.

"Shut up you!"

"Get away from there man!"

"Nincompoop."

While I and the rest of the desperate queue were bent on our enervating struggle, the Big Men, who had generators humming beneath their houses during the power cuts and whose purring slick cars glided over tar as though floating on air, simply strutted in and strutted out with the shop assistants lapping at their feet, pushing trolleys of *mealie-meal* bags after them, two and three and four bags per person.

When I left the deranged crowd the 'controller of the queue' was still yapping with a relentless energy. It was dark and I was slightly bruised. I felt cheated, for the war in which I had fought had only yielded a battle's worth of loot: one bag of *mealie-meal*, which, to my despair, was leaking.

Uncle Tom Died

Farai Godobo

Uncle Tom died. No one wept for him. People seemed happy with his dying. So he just died, and no one wept for him. Uncle Tom was not my uncle, nor were we related in any way. He was 'uncle' because he had no wife, and we lived at the same house. He used one room, and we used three, but he was the owner of the house. None of his relatives were there to see him die, he just confided his death to my frail mind. I understood nothing about death, and when he told me about his death, I took it lightly like the gifts that he so often gave me.

He was a dedicated womaniser. Hardly would a dress pass by without his round eyes stripping the woman naked. He had his peculiar look; a stare that, he told me, disarmed tough women. I do not know where he worked, but after each day's toil he seemed to be awarded a woman for his immense contribution to the working world. His women came in all shapes and sizes: tall and slim, gigantic but soft; he 'tamed' them all.

Uncle Tom had a liking for alcohol and, under his influence, I tasted my first sip of booze. What a stale drink, a pungent drink that burned my throat like eating hot ash! After that experience I vowed never to take alcohol again. He called me FANTA – Foolish Africans Never Take Alcohol, after I had sworn not to drink again. Our conspiratorial intimacy began from there. I was his Fanta and he became my Uncle. Uncle Tom had a wide circle of friends, most bachelors, just like himself. They often came and crowded into his room, making a lot of noise that would drive Mother to the shops. She resented this behaviour but she could do nothing about it. It was his home after all.

After a party with his friends, one by one his women would start to trickle in. He had a pre-planned arrangement, designed in such a way that they never had the chance to meet each other. Mother disliked him using women, he respected her for her age, and he called her Mother, but I called him Uncle all the same.

Things went on like that for as far back as I can remember. Then one weekend he woke with a limp. Curious to know, but with a shallow understanding of the adult world, I asked in my ignorance what the matter was. "I have been bitten" was all he would say. I just kept quiet.

Time passed and Uncle Tom's life slowed down. The number of women who visited him dwindled to a mere trickle, until none came at all. He began to stay home most of the time, and the number of gifts that he gave me decreased. He seemed unhappy, but I was too engrossed in playing to think of his problems.

A conversation we had one day later influenced the path my life would take.

"What grade are you doing, Fanta?"

"Two. And I am being taught by Mrs…"

"I know that. What do you want to be when you grow up?"

"I want to be just like you, and live alone without Mother and Father and…"

"No, no, no. I want you to be a doctor so that you can cure people who are sick like me. If you live alone like me, you will end up sick like me."

My mind was not fertile enough to let those words grow.

"But *Malume*…," I looked around to see if Mother was there, and then continued, "you have many women."

He shook his head sadly at that, but made no comment.

With time Uncle Tom's skin began to darken. Mother told me it was because he sat in the sun too much, but I sensed that she was hiding something from me. She slapped me before telling me that next time I must learn not to get too involved in analysing people's skins. She eventually forbade me to go and watch TV in Uncle Tom's room. That is when I noticed that his friends no longer visited. His sister came once and never returned. Uncle Tom became sick.

He was sitting in the sun outside his room when I came home from school one day. I just greeted him and went to look for something to satisfy my hunger. I was about to go and play when he asked me why I was not coming to watch TV any more. I let the cat out of the bag, and, all of a sudden, he told me that he would die the following day.

The next morning he did not come to sit in the sun. I playfully told Mother that Uncle Tom had said he would die that day. I had never seen Mother alarmed before, but on that day I saw her almost cry. Uncle Tom's death meant that we were to leave Nketa 6. Surely, people do not realise the importance of their behinds until they get a boil. She went to tell Uncle Tom's sister, and later the police came and took his body. There was no funeral, but we were simply told to pack our things and go. No one wept for him, but inwardly I cried for my loss.

Freedom

Bongani Ncube

I jumped.

These are the two most important words of my life because as of that moment they defined the course my life was to take.

Months of indecision – I might jump – I can jump – I will jump. At last it's all in the past. I jumped. There's no changing it now. What's done is done. Cry for the milk that is yet to be spilt. Waste not tears on me. I have jumped. What was just a thought in my mind is now a reality, set in stone, bound by time and the universe…

I jumped…

Twenty-five storeys into the air, with my arms outstretched, as if diving off the springboard at Borrow Street pool. Grabbing at nothing, forsaking the ground that has been my mainstay for the air that will let me go, let me crash into the pavement below, let me fall to my doom, let me die.

I jumped off the side of the N.R.Z. building. Now all I can feel is the air pulling at my clothes, as if trying to pull me back – but it's too late now.

I'm falling like a stone towards the ground, pulled by the invisible strings that bind all of us to the dust from which we came. I go willingly.

Do I sound poetic? Well I wouldn't be surprised because I am a poet. Right now there's a poet-me falling to his death. He isn't doing anything a poet is supposed to be doing: reading, writing and capturing life in ink.

Neither is he doing anything a person is supposed to be doing – eating, laughing, living. If only life were so simple; sticking to the role assigned.

I'm falling. I can't describe how it feels. For once things are going my way, I've finally made a decision no one can change. Nothing can change.

Look at all those people on the ground getting on with life. They are stupid. They have no idea, absolutely no idea how it feels to have willingly let go of all control, to be at the mercy of forces that care not an iota for you. To acknowledge this and revel in the fact.

They think they are in control of their lives. I have let go of all control and now I'm more in control than I've ever felt. Is this how a religious experience feels? Has a bolt of wisdom struck me?

Too late.

Too late to understand. Too late now. Too late to be loved. The ground is rushing up at an incredible speed and it really isn't time to start getting philosophical. Come to think of it, it isn't the best time for anything. It's too late.

Too late to regret.

Or is it?

Too late to claw my way back up through the air, too late to start screaming. Why am I screaming?

Why am I screaming?

Look at them. They are looking at me. They look shocked, amazed. They're wondering why anyone in their right mind would jump off a twenty-five-storey building.

I think I am wondering as well.

What am I doing?

I'm falling.

Why?

I jumped.

Why did I jump? *WHY* did I jump? Look, I've made a mess of my life again. I'm useless. Everything I do is a mistake. I've jumped off a building for crying out loud. I'm going to hit the ground at a very high speed. I'm going to crash into the ground. Soon. Very soon. The ground won't give way, I will.

Don't think I'm stupid. It's just that I really didn't think beyond the fact that I would jump. Didn't think I would have to think about it as I hurtled towards the ground.

Calm down.

Calm down. This is your suicide, don't ruin even that, you've already ruined your life.

What am I saying?

That has got to be the most ridiculous thing I've ever said. I should

52

remember this so I can tell...

WHO?

Who am I going to tell?

The devil? My ancestors? Where am I going? What am I doing? What have I done?

Too late.

When You Look At Me

Sonia Chidakwa

Hear me please
I don't mean to bother you,
I just want to air my views too.
You look down on me.
Oh! I see, when you look at me
My point will be invalid, you won't listen,
You see a sorrowful sight,
My opinions are disabled.

Well, I don't care
I'll speak my mind,
I just want to destroy the wall you are closing me in.
You are astounded, why so?
Oh! I see when you look at me
You only expect to hear a pitiful story.

Dear me,
You're stuck with your old notions,
Update your mind.
When you look at me
You read the label, Double D, "Disabled and Daft".
Are you so backdated
That you still watch black and white screens
When the real world is beautiful with all its colours?
What is a human being without a mind, a spirit and a body?
And I have them all.
Yet when you look at me
It seems I am alienated.
Touch me and see if I am contagious,
Talk to me and hear if I babble,
Look at me and tell me
What is inhuman in me.

Heartbeats

Babusi Nyoni

As MaiMuripo pounded the millet her frail heart pounded with it. Harder and harder with each stroke. And with each stroke a tear fell. Exploding as it hit the ground into even tinier droplets. Moistening the dust, slowly. She stopped for a second and pulled up her apron to wipe the waters of emotion from her face. "Gogo, what's wrong?" asked Shuvai, tugging at the hem of her grandmother's yellow dress. "Nothing my dear," she managed to say between sobs, "go see if the porridge is ready."

Why it had to be her daughter still puzzled her. She stood with her arms akimbo and the pestle resting against her shoulder, looking at nothing but trying so hard to see it. She swatted a fly that had ventured too close to her grain and returned, once more, to her pose. Netsai had been such a zesty young girl before. Now she was just a lethargic bag of miserable bones. No longer the gem of her village. At the most, just a speck. But she was not always like this. Before leaving for Harare she had every man at her feet, begging her for her ever-so-rarely-given attention. She left in the green bus that always played a melody with its horn as it left the rank. *Sekuru* Mathias gave her round nuts to eat on the journey and MaiMuripo roasted her a chicken and prepared *samp* for her meal. Aunt Moira gave her a red dress she had made with a pattern of intricate red polka dots and delicate lace trimmings she had taken from another garment. She travelled well, meeting more relations who gave her more gifts and advice on the ills and joys of city life. She only sent one letter and that was the letter describing her journey. That was the last they heard of her until she came back. No longer what she had been.

MaiMuripo lifted the pestle and laid it on the mat. She undid the knot of her *m'zambiya* and retied it. Lambs bleated under the white glare of the October sun and heat waves distorted the skyline. The baobab tree to the west stood framed against a cloudless sky. Acacia pods exploded spewing seeds onto the hardened earth and crickets filled the sluggish setting with their sound. The cattle boys reclined, sprawled under the shade of the msasa tree with their home-made whips in a bundle not far from them. Flies drifted from hut to hut. MaiMuripo walked to the well, her cracked feet searing each time they touched the baked ground. The wind lifted dust, tainting an already filthy sky. She crooked her arm to try to shield her eyes from the dust and soldiered on.

When she got to the well she sat on its edge and tried to catch her breath.

"Why my daughter, why?" she screamed at an unseen entity and sat gazing at the sky as though expecting a response. Tears welled in her eyes. The jingle of cow-bells could be heard in the distance. She looked to see whose they were but tears blurred her vision, she saw nothing. She blindly tugged at the rope pulling the bucket and emptied the silted water into her clay jug and let the bucket fall back in. She heard the far away splash it made as it hit the water.

She walked back to the homestead, precariously balancing the jug on her head as she faced the fury of the near-setting sun. To the north she could hear the faint braying of donkeys and the echoing bark of her eldest son's dogs. She unlatched the wooden gate and trudged on to the kitchen where she laid the jug down and waited for the sand to settle.

Netsai feebly waved her emaciated arm as she tried to swipe an overzealous mosquito. She had been woken by the rattle of the door in the wind and was finding it difficult to fall asleep again. Eyes half closed, she pushed the blanket off her body and struggled to get up. She used the chair for leverage and propped herself against the wall in a slumped position. Shuvai, her only daughter, would probably not see many more birthdays and it was all because of her. She wept and her tears flowed onto her lips.

MaiMuripo gently knocked on the door. "Are you awake Netsai?" she asked and kept silent in anticipation of an answer. The door creaked open as Netsai opened it, her hand on the adjacent wall for support. Her mother stood there stunned, for a brief moment pondering whether her daughter was on the road to recovery.

"Mother, I have something I want to say to you. I don't have a spirit inside of me..." she managed to say haltingly as she sat back on the bed. "All I have is… it's AIDS mama."

Wind rustled the thatch and a line of ants scurried in a straight line across the ground. Tumbleweed bounced along on the dust-road. The cattle boys dusted the backs of their shorts as they stood up to bring the cattle home. The go-away bird was silent. The water jug slipped from MaiMuripo's hands and shattered as it hit the ground.

MaiMuripo knelt down and tried to gather the shards of the broken clay vessel that now lay on the wet earthen floor. Her daughter helped her. They were silent.

"Please say something, Mother," Netsai pleaded as she sat on the bed.

MaiMuripo moved to sit beside her daughter. "I knew already," she said.

Netsai was stunned. For how long had the old woman known?

Her mother spoke again. "I just wanted to hear it from you, that's all. Your food is getting cold. Eat up and Shuvai will bring you a drink."

MaiMuripo sat there and watched her daughter eat.

It started to rain.

Mental Footpaths

Michael Hove

Humans are born blank sheets of paper upon which their destiny is written until the pages of their lives are all set down. The pages of my life have a dominant theme of alienation. I'm an orphan. Do you think I don't have parents? Well you're wrong. I do have parents. But parents are parents because of their expected roles. Mine have given me everything except love. I guess I simply have biological parents. Let me tell you something you don't know about my life. I have my own room full of pictures of beautiful women and celebrities. I go to one of the coolest schools in the country. I have a *Playstation 3*, an *X Box 360*, a mountain bike, a laptop with internet access. My clothes are all designer wear. I have more pocket money than the pages of my mathematics textbook. I have it all. It's all mine but yet it really isn't. I can easily lose it. But still, I just have it all. But it's just that four letter word my parents can't spell out to me. Love. I'm looking for love, not material things.

Instead of these material things bringing me closer to my parents, they in fact pull me away from them. They buy them to cheat me. It's like taking a toddler to hospital to be cured of an illness. The child feels the excruciating pain as the injection sinks into her buttocks. The only thing to silence the loud, deafening cry of the toddler is to give it that sweet you have bought along in advance, knowing the after effects of the painful spike. But what good is the sweet? As soon as the child discovers that it can no longer taste the sweetness it will cry again, this time louder. The sweet is like opium. It makes things seem as if they are not the way they are, when in fact they are the way they are, and such is my life with these beautiful things around me.

The material possessions do not provide the love I seek in my relationship with my parents. Ours is a relationship void of love.

I'll tell you this. I hope you relate to it. It's around seven o'clock. Me, my two sisters and my mother are in the sitting room watching television. Everyone is waiting for *Generations* to start, our favourite South African soap. We are all happy. We are having supper, which is okay, but in the wrong venue. It is taboo to have supper in the sitting room in this family, but today it's okay, Father is not yet in. This happiness won't last long, I feel it down my spine. It's not normal for everyone to be happy in this family. Just when *Generations* is about to start no mouth asks any ear whether it has heard the *Land Rover* approaching from a distance. By instinct, everyone knows what to do. Even the cockroaches have heard it. Haphazardly they scurry all over in search of shelter – under the breadbin and cupboards, screaming "take cover, take cover". In seconds everything is in abnormal order once again. Everyone heads straight to bed to pretend they have been sleeping for ages. The sofas are left watching *Generations*. They will tell us what transpired the next day. The moment Father steps in the house fear grips everyone. The heavy sound of throbbing hearts from under the blankets alerts him that something suspect has been happening. He marches in to the sitting room and immediately notices a few grains of rice on the carpet. He summons Mother for interrogation. He stares at her but she cannot look back. His piercing eyes would see into her skull, creating a wound that would never heal. At this point, silence rules. It's as if someone has just died, but even where there is death there is loud wailing and crying, but this silence has no definition, yet it has been there for years. Sometimes I wish my father was a drunkard, so that when he came home from work he would collapse in to bed. Too bad he's always sober twenty-four-seven. But maybe things might just be worse. Who knows?

After having his supper he calls me. He asks me rhetorical questions. "Do you think you are the owner of this house? Do you think you are now a grown up? In your own house you can have supper in the sitting room, not in my house, is that understood?" The tremor-hit reply faintly escapes my shivering throat, "Ye... ye... yes." So, Mother told him that it was me, and only me, enlarging my belly in the sitting room. I think she hates men. She hates Father and me too. She thinks that when I grow up and develop that ugly kinky beard, I too will treat her badly. The conversation with my father does not end there. The unfriendly conclusion is rescheduled to his bedroom where the sound of the ironing cord is heard. I look like a zebra. The stripes on my body show the traces of my father's whip dancing on my body. The good news is that I can no longer feel pain, it's like an adrenaline rush. I think he knows it too. He's threatened to introduce a new dancer, a knobkerrie. That way I will be thoroughly disciplined.

I fear that one day he will kill me or throw me out. He would certainly chase me away if he heard that I'd impregnated a girl. I feel he is eagerly awaiting the moment when I make a mistake that would ruin my life. But he does not know that I'm careful. I don't think I could cope with life on the streets. I am not ready to be hugged by the arms of street dustbins. I honestly don't know where I would go. At least at home I get clothed, fed and schooled. Who on earth would take care of me? But yet... perhaps life on the streets would be better than what I'm experiencing right now, this loveless life.

"Students, there's a theme of reincarnation in this novel. You just have to..." Reincarnation! This word wakes me up the next day in the middle of a literature lesson as the teacher explains. What if I were reincarnated? Born in a different country, family, with a different name, face, thoughts and feelings. To be born with a completely new identity. Would that be better than life on the streets? I've thought about suicide. But why? Is it worth it for me to kill myself because of someone else? Just to make him feel guilty for the pain that he has caused me. To drench that Sahara-like face wet with tears. To make him grieve for a soul that is going to come back and haunt him and make his nights miserable. I don't think so! The pages of my life are not yet over. Ahead of me is a footpath that has grown no grass, waiting for me to journey on it till the very edges of the Earth. Whoever is writing the script of my life, I want the concluding chapters to tell of an old man with white hair, who has lived a long life filled with the love that I've not yet had, not even from my mother. I want to find a home, not a house. I will move on and on, determination pushing me forward. I'm an orphan, seeking love.

The Tale of an African Forest

Lee Hlalo

One day, during a stroll with his mother, Tonderai stumbled upon something; it was a huge stump right in the middle of the forest. The inquisitive boy started investigating the stump, trying to find anything interesting about it, when suddenly he discovered a queer looking root coming out of the ground. On approaching the root it said, "Here lie the remains of Deidre Baobab", then it kept quiet. He wanted it to go on talking about Deidre Baobab, so he begged his mother to try and make it go on. His mother, very familiar with ancient customs, knew what to do; she simply went to the root and tapped it twice and it began telling the story of Deidre Baobab. The baffled boy wanted to ask a question but held his words back, in fear of disrupting the magical root, as he had come to think of it.

This is how the story was told:

"I am Deidre Baobab and these are my memoirs. I lived in the Wooflen Forest and enjoyed it there. Summer, although very hot and tiring, was a very pleasing time to me, with all the hustle and bustle of the local birds and squirrels in the woods, forever going up and down my branches all day long. The forest was always bustling with excitement and I enjoyed the company of my tenants and all the sounds they made, however queer!

"Then there was the delightful time when the forest played host to the ever charming swallows, the black and white parade as it has been dubbed. We had a lovely time catering to the visitors, mixing in a bit of sport, as Mrs Marula, Mrs Msasa and I had a competition on who would have the most tenants, as the swallows were a picky bunch, but nonetheless I always turned out the victor every year, as the swallows preferred the big build of us

Baobabs! Ah! Yes, summer was one of my favourite seasons.

"With autumn came the inevitable goodbye to our summer visitors as they set off on their long journey. How sad, but life went on.

"The inhabitants of the forest were busy in summer, but more so in autumn as they prepared for the winter ahead. It was an enjoyable time of year for me, watching the squirrels run to and fro looking for berries and nuts on which to feed as they hibernated. I found amusement in watching them squabble for food.

"Mr Oaktree would always complain of headaches due to the woodpecker that lived in his head always making new holes.

"Mrs Acacia complained about Mr Owl who used to keep her up at night, with his obsessive interrogation of all the other birds. He used to have a secret stash of nuts stored away somewhere, returning one day to find it gone. He went mad trying to look for it. From that day onwards all he could say was "who who who". I thought Mr Owl was one of the most interesting characters in the forest.

"Mr Teak, Mrs Msasa and Mr and Mrs Marula were fortunate enough to have well mannered tenants who did not get on their nerves.

"With all the preparations done, then came the really fun part of autumn. The Wooflen Ball. Of course there could be no dancing but all the trees of Wooflen Forest sure did dress up. It was a festival of colours, with all the trees sporting a new colour: Mrs Marula displaying a lavish moss dress, Mrs Msasa a lovely burnt brown attire, and I an extravagant velvet purple. Even the forest floor couldn't be outdone as it sported a carpet of golden leaves. The animals joined the festivities by producing the music for which they were renowned. That day was certainly a day to remember.

"As the cruel winter drew closer we had to say goodbye to most of the forest folk as they were going into hibernation. The forest then was as dead as a doorknob, all hush, with only a few trees swaying from side to side, and the whistling of the cold winter winds. Oh how I dreaded winter!

"I knew that spring had at last arrived when I heard the chatter of the playful squirrels. I stretched my branches up into the air as if awakening from a deep slumber.

"As the morning dew dripped off my tender leaves I thought of how beautiful I had become. My flowers were in full bloom, and the scent was extraordinary. I might not have been much of a sight for most of the year, but in spring I was the envy of everyone. I loved spring because it was my time to shine, it brought out the star in me.

"Spring didn't do this just for me, but for everyone else in the forest; the trees and the animals all put their best foot forward, as there were flowers and shiny new coats to be flaunted. Oh, there was nothing like a Wooflen Forest Spring, what joy it brought."

With that the root paused and after a while continued, "All was well until Man came to conquer the Wooflen Forest, and all that could be heard was the clitter clatter of Man's terrible machines. One by one my friends fell to the ground, until they were all gone!

"On the fateful day that they came for me, I gathered up all my strength and concentrated it on storing these precious memories. After accomplishing this, they came and with a loud thud the last of the Wooflen trees was gone."

With that the root was silent and the story ended. The boy and his mother were at a loss for words, each one looking like they had something to say but unable to get the words out of their mouths. Moved by the story Tenderai's mother told the touching story to the rest of the villagers. They agreed to stop further construction on that land and to replant so that Wooflen Forest could exist again.

Sadly, this is the story of many African forests that is never heard and these are the memories of the trees that are cut down but never replanted. The beauty of the African continent is beginning to fade as it gives way to rampant development. Day by day her natural beauty disappears. Gone are the days, gone are the days of a natural Africa, gone but not forgotten.

If Only I Could Tell You

Nobuhle Maphosa

The horizon looked so beautiful
from where I stood,
seeing the crow create
a short time silhouette
and the dew that fell
sweetly from the green leaves.
If only I could tell you.

The wood chopped from
the jacarandas fell clumsily
on the quiet road,
while the rustling of the
dry leaves being swept
by the wind
rose quickly.
If only I could tell you.

The horizon began to fade away.
The beginning of my departure
away from where I stood
was so sudden.
If only I could tell you
how beautiful the morning was.

If Only

Rebecca Dube

I can see my dear Mom sobbing bitterly. Her eyes are filled with the suffering and the agony she is going through right now as she is looking into the coffin. I feel an unbearable pain in my heart when I think that the hell she is now in is all because of me. As long as she lived she wasn't going to forgive me. I try to call her but she does not hear my voice. I want to ask for forgiveness for all the things I have done. If only I could have another chance to live, to correct every mistake that I had made, but no, I am wrong, because that would be building a castle in the air. All I want at this moment is to hold her hand and tell her we will meet again one day, but I don't have the strength.

I struggle to stand up, but I am dead and lying in my beautiful casket. I am not going to be resurrected. She passes and takes a last look before she falls on her knees with tears streaming down her cheeks. I recall the day I saw scars on her body and knew, without being told, that it was because of me being pregnant at the young age of fourteen. My father had beaten her because he thought that she should have better advised me of the dangers of sex. My mother had tried her best to take care of me but I was stubborn. All the pain she was going through was my fault.

I think of the day I brought the news of my HIV status home; it was as though I had killed her. She couldn't eat or drink, not to mention her sleepless nights. My father chased her from our house but later forgave her. Recalling those times is as though somebody has stabbed me with a knife in my heart. The pain I feel at this moment is more than words can say. My desperate wish is to stand up and give my mother a hug to comfort her, but it is impossible; there is no turning back.

The next person to pass by to view me in my coffin is my father, my most cruel father. I blame him for the upbringing that made us fear rather than respect him. We were always in a cage as if we were animals. I take a look in his eyes and think I see hatred, but at the same time fear. Of course, he feared that my sister would follow in my footsteps. Seeing tears run down his cheeks makes me cry too. I don't know how I feel, I am all mixed up, just like I was in life. I try to shout and tell him that I am sorry but he doesn't hear my voice. Why does nobody hear me shout at the top of my voice? Perhaps they want me dead after all, because if they don't they are surely supposed to hear me. Despite the pity stirring in my heart for my Dad, I will never forget all the cruel things he did to me. I recall the moment he showed me the door when he learnt I had tested positive. How he hated me! Why is he now crying, pretending he is heartbroken? At least he can now preach his sermons without the stigma of a daughter dying of AIDS. All he seemed to care about was what other people were going to say. Now he can preach and say I was a good, respectful, well-behaved girl, which I wasn't. People say good things about someone when that person is dead, instead of telling the truth. He is a pastor who always wants to paint a good picture of his family. I was tired of being told that I was cursed and was never going to enter the Kingdom of Heaven. Playing, walking, eating, learning … were all about the good black book. We were not allowed to associate with our neighbours' children because he thought that they would teach us wrong things. Serves him right then! He wanted us to dance according to his tune. If only I could turn back the hands of time and tell him that children have to be given some freedom in order to be responsible. I too fear that my sister is going to die the same way. I struggle to get up but I can't!

My dear sister appears. Oh my God! She is sobbing because she has lost me. She treasured the moments we spent together. We cried and laughed together since early childhood. She was always there for me when I needed her, and was my shoulder to lean on. Of course, when she heard the devastating news of my status, she was shocked but was then my pillar of strength. When I was sick she washed and fed me. I want to say I am sorry for being a burden to her but she would not hear me. Seeing her like this makes me weep too. If only I could have another chance to live, to go back to those short but treasured moments we used to share. She cries till she can cry no more, and then stumbles away.

My daughter! For God's sake I can't take this any more! I want to live just for her and watch her grow to become a beautiful woman. She is the most precious little thing to me. She is crying, yes of course, because she has lost her mother. So young and beautiful, she is going to face this cruel world with no parents to help her. I feel pity for her and I am sobbing bitterly now. I long to give her one last big hug, to hold her in my arms, never to let go of her. I love her so very much and never want her to follow in my footsteps. All I want is for her to become an intelligent, hardworking young woman. If only I had talked to her properly before my death. I kept my secret from her and never told her why I am here today. Right now I want to ask for her forgiveness and to show her how much I love her. I hope that when she is older she will understand and that she will forgive me for leaving her. I try to hold her hand, but I can't. She disappears from view.

Other family members pass by one by one. I can see that most of them are heartbroken. Maybe some of them are just crying for the sake of appearances. Some of them resented me when I was still alive, especially my aunty because she thought I was a burden to my parents. I'm sure she encouraged my father to throw me out. Perhaps she will celebrate today that their burden has been removed and thank the Almighty!

If only I could go back to those days I wasted to correct the mistakes I made. I thought I was so clever, showing my family I could do whatever I wanted. All I want now is to live again, to love and be loved, to respect my body. All I want is peace with my family. The viewing ends and my coffin lid is closed. I shout and yell that they cannot leave me in this dark, cold place. Alone in my casket, all I can think is: "If only I could have another chance to live."

Wasted Years

Faith Tshuma

I grew up in a poor community. At that time, back in the years when it was Southern Rhodesia, everyone around me seemed keen to get a good education. I didn't believe in it. I didn't believe that education was the stepping stone to a better life.

Lying under a msasa tree outside my dilapidated homestead, I allow my mind to take me back to my past life. I'm filled with regret, pity for myself and a sombreness in my heart. My wife and children are suffering. I wish I could turn back the hands of time.

My son approaches me. His clothes are tattered. Pain rushes through my heart. I realise that I'm to blame for my family's predicament. Back in those early days, being poor seemed natural. We shared the same experiences and grievances. Thoughts race through my mind like mice in a dark tunnel. I ask myself what can a poor, illiterate man do to get money? My son says something to me. I smile, but I fail to figure out what he has said.

"Father, I'm speaking to you and you are not answering. What's wrong? You don't seem to be yourself," he says, trying to draw a response from me.

I look at him and see that everything is wrong. Everyone around can see that his trousers are torn. I spend most of my time in the fields, chopping firewood, working hard. Are other men busier or more hardworking than myself? Are those who work in the city better able to provide for their families? Why has everything turned out like this?

I manage to say something to him. "Son, I am like this today because I refused to be someone back then. What you do today will determine your tomorrow. Don't ever fool yourself by saying you are going to be a wise man tomorrow. You must be a wise boy now."

The expression on his face shows me that he is puzzled. I realise that it is time I told my story to my only son. I had named him Hope in the belief that he would have a better life, that things would be different for him.

"Boy, you never know what life will bring. Everything now is viewed through Eurocentric, city eyes. I chose the rural African way – but look at me now."

"Dad, it seems like the past made you like this. Was it your fault, or your family, your parents?" he asked with a tremor in his voice.

My mind flashes back to my past. I knew from long back that my family blamed me for everything. It is a disgrace to them that the family do not have a home in the city. They have never even been there. When I raise my eyebrows, my son is looking straight into my eyes. I try to evade his look. I cannot bear the word pain reflected in them.

Again I allow my memory to take me back to my childhood, when my father was still alive. He had a vision of me being a highly educated son. He called me to bring home-brewed beer to quench his thirst after a long day's work in the white man's fields. I heard his voice echo behind me: "Son, are you sure that you have taken the right decision by not continuing to go to school? Can't you see that to live a better life you need to follow what the white men have done? This education that you ignore today will be necessary tomorrow. Don't look back in later life and blame me, it will have been your own fault if you do not go to school. But it's your choice."

I remember I used to feel like a warrior who had conquered simply because I had manipulated my father to allow me to have my way. My friends from school used to call me a 'stupid fool' for not staying on, but in turn I would say, "Who are the stupid ones?" With that the conversation would turn to laughter. As time went by, they stopped bothering me with their irritating talk.

My Dad always did everything I wanted, everything to help me. He even paid the *lobola* with his own cattle for my beautiful and loving wife. After our marriage, everything was spick and span for many years... until I lost my parents. I then had to move to build my own homestead. A black cloud of reality fell over me. I had to face this unbearable world on my own as a father of five.

Seeing my educated friends who had gone to the city prosper, I then decided to catch a bus to the 'City of Kings' to try my luck. I had envied the jobs and the salaries that my friends had, but the employment I could get was inferior to theirs in every way. With time, I realised it was because of their education. When I went back to the village for the first time to visit, I decided never to go back to the city. My wife tried to convince me to keep trying, that my luck would change. "My husband, do you know that there is a star for every man in the sky?"

Those words touched me, but I told her that I was the only one on this planet without a star. The city had been unwelcoming. I found life there unbearable. As a traditional family man, I didn't want to spend my evenings drinking beer in hotels and nightclubs with my friends, who seemed to be having the time of their lives with those beautiful young 'spring chickens' of the night. I would never allow my daughters to explore the city because to me it seemed that all the young women there from the rural areas could not think of anything except 'money and men'.

The moment I decided to stay in the rural areas with my family I knew that life would never be the same again. I knew it would not offer anything good to me. In sixteen years of marriage, I had never known my wife to be so depressed. My decision to stay in the village seemed to torment her; she felt that people began to mock our poverty.

"Peace," I said to her one night. "Our neighbours enjoy it when we are suffering and they never bother to offer a helping hand, even though they say do good to others for you don't know what the future holds."

Together we should have been strong, never to be shaken, and be able to plan the future of our kids together. Despite the hard times we have had, I know I have to work hard and strive to give my children a good education so that they won't be a laughing stock like their father, but will be the redeemers of the family. I will keep the spirit for the sake of my children and be a good father to them.

After telling Hope the story of my past, I look at him. He is obviously moved, with tears streaming down his face, as he says, "You can't stop the birds from flying over your head, but you can stop them from making a nest in your hair. Those were wasted years. You can't do anything about them. It's all in the past. But the future lies ahead of me, I can learn from your past mistakes."

I feel drained. Sweating like a schoolboy who has run for miles, I raise my head and smile at him. Now he understands.

Tears

Novuyo Rosa Tshuma

Have you ever seen your father cry? A father you had never seen cry, who had always stood as a man among the rest, crumble before your eyes? Baba cried the day Thabo came home. He cried tears that seemed like they would never dry, that fell from his face with the fury of the summer rains that cursed the ground with each drop. He cried and I trembled, because something terrible had to happen now, something more terrible than Thabo.

I remember I was in the kitchen, crouched over the pot of soya porridge throbbing gently on the fire. It had rained the night before and I hadn't brought in the firewood, and the logs were steaming into my eyes, fighting the weak flames of the fire.

But it was a beautiful November morning, the aroma of wet soil permeating the air, the dew pressing the renewed grass to the ground, the earth heavy with the promise of fecundity. I was battling with the fire when the scream cut through my head. Mama's scream. I was out of the kitchen in a flash, skidding all over the compound until I saw Mama by the cart beneath the pawpaw tree, tearing at her clothes and rolling on the ground, hurling deathly screams that made my skin crawl.

At first I couldn't recognise the puss infected, skeletal figure heaped up in the cart. Then I stumbled backwards, horrified. "No... no..."

My eyes searched the compound, the dirt road disappearing into the cluster of mopane trees, searched for something that they knew they would not see. Where was the big white car that would make a deafening 'vroom vroom' sound, that would upset the dust with the ferocity of the July winds, the one Baba said had big cushioned leather seats and a booming stereo? The one he bragged about to anyone who would listen, using all the big words that were written in impressive handwriting in Thabo's letter? He had even gone on to pinch an ear or two about his elevated status; he was sure that Thabo's achievements would better his chances of getting elected to the Council.

No, it couldn't be Thabo. Thabo was big now, tall and fat, from the burgers and cottage pies and pizzas and exotic dishes he never failed to mention in his letters. He was the blessed one, the chosen one, the one who had won the 'The World a Global Village' scholarship to university, then crossed the seas to the white man's land, and returned with a degree. Your eyes would swell as Baba said this, rolled the word *degree* off his tongue with the delicate handling of an egg, weighed you down with the importance of it. It made you understand just how great Thabo now was, how he was one of the special people, the important people who got into university, and came out holding a degree. I had always thought Thabo was lying, that there could not be such a place as America. I would stare at pictures of the Statue of Liberty, the crazy tall glass buildings, the roads that criss-crossed each other and even went beneath the ground, the trains that passed through the city, the breathtaking buildings of the university, and a very chubby Thabo, grinning at the camera, an arm slung across the shoulders of a pretty white girl with long hair the colour of the sun and shiny eyes the colour of the sky. I would spend hours taking all this in, trying, but finding it very difficult to fathom.

Secretly, I wished to see the place for myself one day, to also get a 'The World a Global Village' scholarship to America. But Baba would never waste money educating a girl. What did a woman need school for? Too much school, Mama said, spoiled a woman. Her head got too big and she would begin to talk back to her husband. Did you need school to make soft smooth *sadza* and spicy *amangqina* over the fire? Did you need school to get a husband? No, she spat, drops of saliva landing on my face, it was enough to know how to read and write. I nodded solemnly, not knowing what else to do. Already they were talking about my *lobola*. But in my wildest of dreams I saw myself there. I would seek the shade of the orange trees clustered near Mama's hut, and dream of myself among all those important people at university, touching a white man, holding a degree. Just like Thabo.

It was the white men, Baba decided. They had poisoned his son with their white *muti*. It was that old man Dambo, who wanted the Council seat for himself. It was Uncle Fiso, who was telling everyone that Baba was nothing but an old fat goat who didn't even know what a steering wheel was. It was anyone and everyone.

Mama lashed out at Mama BoyBoy. She was the one trying to kill Thabo, so that, as the second wife, her son would be eligible to inherit Baba's fields and his goats and his cattle. "You witch, witch!" Mama screeched, sucking her finger and swiping at the air, a promise of vengeance. "You think you have me, eh, you think you have me!" And she began to rip her clothes off. "I will embarrass you today, today I will embarrass you." She continued until she was stark naked, and then followed Mama BoyBoy wherever she went. "Take me then, eh, take me! Kill me, like you have killed my son, take me."

I tried to console Mama, told her not to worry, she had me. But she said I did not count. I was a woman. I would inherit nothing, would go off somewhere one day to make fertile the house of another clan. She cursed the ancestors for having given her the seed of only two children, having turned their back on her identity, her son.

I was afraid to approach Thabo, to speak my mind. I went into Mama's hut where he lay, pinching my face at the stench of sickness that clenched the room, dumbstruck at the king who had fallen from his throne. I tried not to see how red the blisters were against his black skin, how pink his lips, how grotesque the eyes in that sunken face.

"Is it... is it AIDS?"

I didn't know that I had said the words out loud until he lashed out at me. "I don't have AIDS man!" His lips were curled up in a grimace. "I'm sick of this stupid AIDS business. Whenever anyone is sick, it's AIDS! Aren't you tired of it? AIDS AIDS AIDS! Is that all you can think of?"

I faltered. I had never seen Thabo like this before. He was trembling now, his whole body shivering like he had a fever.

"Is that all they teach you at school, to go around accusing every sick person of having AIDS? And why are you still at school? You want to turn into one of those silly women who think that because they are educated now, they can wear the trousers in the house? Screaming 'infidelity' and flinging divorce in my face, there's nothing like infidelity where I come from – ."

He caught himself, blinked repeatedly, as though awakening from a trance. I stepped back slowly, my focus on the precious little light forcing itself through the window. America died in my heart that day.

"It's as Mama says," he said, calmly now. "I've been cursed. It's why I'm here. People are jealous and I've been cursed."

I nodded repeatedly. "Yes," I whispered. "Yes."

Yes. Thabo couldn't have AIDS. Thabo was the chosen one. Mama had said once, when the officials from the World Health Organisation came, that she wished antiretrovirals had never been created, so that we would all know who had been prostituting themselves in our midst, and fix them. I remember the way she said that word, 'fix', with such venom that Aunty Prissy cringed, didn't go forward to collect the free ARVs. No, it wasn't ARVs I had seen in Thabo's bag, because Thabo did not, could not, have AIDS. Thabo was the chosen one, the blessed one. The one who had come home with a degree.

If a Dog was the Teacher

Leanne Quinche

If a dog was the teacher, you would learn stuff like:

When your loved ones return you always run and greet them.
Never pass up an opportunity to go on a joyride.
Allow the experience of wind and fresh air in your face to be pure ecstasy.
When it's in your best interests practise obedience.
Let others know when they've invaded your territory.
Avoid biting when a simple growl will do.
Whenever scolded, don't buy into the guilt and pout,
run right back and make friends.
Delight in the simple joy of a long walk.
Be loyal, never pretend to be something you're not.
If what you want lies buried, dig until you find it.
When someone is having a bad day, be silent,
sit close by and nuzzle them gently.

What You Did Not Read in the Headline

Thembelihle Zulu

Soneni stared wide-eyed, her eyes glazed over with hunger, at the gloomy picture of her children eating water. She wondered how long she could keep going. Her mouth watered at the sight of the bone she had boiled to make the meal. She had been boiling the same bone for the past three nights, but it still looked appetising to her. She licked her white chapped lips to console her taste buds. Her children looked up at her, and even though they thanked her for the meal, their eyes gave away their longing for more. They got up and tidied the plates away because they knew there would be no more food that day. Guilt, anger and resentment saturated Soneni's every cell. Hunger, fatigue and desperation ravaged through her like lightning across a cloud, but only one tear fell.

That night, she tossed and turned on the cold floor, wondering if she could sink any lower. Her helplessness kept her from sleeping, her hungry stomach kept her from gathering her thoughts, and her resentment at her late husband kept her from even thinking of loving again. Only her kids kept her from giving up. An orphan herself, the thought of her children being without a mother and a father was unthinkable to Soneni.

The sleepless night finally came to an end. Her heart fell at the thought of the beginning of yet another day. She knew every day was a battle and today would be no different. Her existence in this famine-stricken country was bleak. Famine was no longer an article in the newspaper. Hunger had become her life. It was all she could think of, it was her every breath and at every blink of her eyes she remembered the hunger in her household.

As she sat at her desk in her classroom she saw a face that she recognised, the face of hunger, staring at her from every child in her class. She imagined how many other parents were in a similar situation to her own. Soneni loved her job, but found it hard to teach on an empty stomach, and neither could the children learn when they were so hungry. Her passion for teaching did not put food on the table; her monthly salary was hardly enough for one loaf of bread. She loved the feeling of making a difference in children's lives, but even this pleasure was taken from her at the thought of her malnourished children. She dismissed her class not a moment too soon and gathered her belongings. No matter how much she hated going home, she hated being away from her kids even more.

She awoke that night with a start. She knew what she had to do. They had to go. There was no money to pay the landlord. She packed their necessities and woke her children very early. The children followed her in the half-light as they trudged into the town. On reaching their destination, she went to the bank to withdraw the little money that she had. The family then sat down on the pavement to sell the few pieces of jewellery she had and all their spare clothes. All that remained for them to carry was one small bag. The time had come for them to start their long journey southwards. They began to walk until the children ceased to chatter.

After several days of walking, they reached the border town. The children watched as their mother approached a shady figure to whom she spoke in hushed tones. The conversation ended in nods and handshakes. Soneni ran back to her children and gathered them around her to hug them and to tell them how much she loved them and how what they were about to do was all for the best. She led them to the edge of the river and kissed them like she would never see them again. They waded into the cold, murky water.

Soneni knew the dangers that lurked within these waters and that with every step she was putting all their lives in danger. She reached the far riverbank first and helped her children stagger onto the bank. They all fell into a pile like dirty laundry but there was no time to waste. She got up, praised them for their bravery and told them that they still had a long way to go. With one last glance at the river and the country they were leaving behind, they walked on into the world of the unknown.

The children had never seen such a fence before but they had come too far to turn back now. They saw other people running towards the barrier and struggling over the barbed wire. This had to be done quickly; there was no time to waste. Their mother encouraged them and some other border jumpers even paused in their flight to help the family. Many others had opted to leave their children behind, but Soneni could not do this. When the children were safely through, their helpers scurried in different directions like prisoners after a jailbreak.

After talking to others escaping their plight in their homeland, the family made their way to a squatter camp near Johannesburg. Soneni used up the little money that she had to buy food and a few materials for a basic shelter. After eating, they picked out a spot in the crowded squatter camp and began building their new home. It was shabby but it was home. Their first home in the land of opportunity. She assured the children that this was the beginning of great things to come. They explored the camp and met many people just like themselves. They heard stories of the fellow border jumpers who had not made it across the river and stories of the wounded seeking refuge in this neighbouring country.

A warm feeling pulsed through her body; she knew she was blessed to be here. She sat on a bench with her children and buried her head in her hands and began to pray. She expressed her gratitude to the God she served and thanked her ancestors for all her blessings and asked for guidance into the future. The depression she had felt was now history; surely there were only good things to come. She cried tears of joy and, with every tear, a bad memory was erased. It was the calm after troubled waters.

She rushed into their shelter smiling from ear to ear and hugged her kids. She squeezed them as tightly as she could. She had reason to celebrate, she had heard of the possibility of a job from another woman who lived nearby. She sent her children out to fetch water and she began making a fire. Her melodious humming was interrupted by the sound of chanting. She rushed out to investigate and saw a horde of people armed with torches. She dropped her pot and rushed to find her children. As she ran, the squatters around her began to stampede. In their panic they knocked her down, into the path of the oncoming angry mob. They were upon her before she was able to get up and, in the mayhem that ensued, her dress caught fire. She screamed for help and reached out, but in vain, no one was willing to help her. Her death became a headline in the reporting of the xenophobic attacks. But the headline did not tell the story of Soneni's life.

Borderline Birth

Gamila Elmaadawy

"We didn't think she could make it," the Officer murmured, as he shook his head in wonder.

The girl cut through the night air, falling and tripping, the bloodhounds at her heels. Her panting filled my ears. Our racing hearts jumped at each anguished scream. Not even the jagged stones under her aching feet had mercy. Blood thundered in my eardrums.

Suddenly there was silence. She crouched down, struggling to muffle her own breath. Her body trembled violently to the core, cowering against the rough trunk of a generous baobab. Far off came the rumble of a truck and the low voices of border police. She sat in semi-darkness, with only the stars' feeble light to comfort. There was no longer the consoling weight of her purse in her pocket, its emptiness had left her destitute. She was now alone, abandoned by her guide, so close to the border. But she was undeterred, despite the sleepless nights, the bush, the filth and the pain. She did not want to return to the place of her birth where she saw no future. Pain shot to her abdomen. She had chosen this way out – saving up a fortune to pay traffickers and conquer the Limpopo.

The shock of cold water reached me, as she lifted her dress and waded in to the river. Thoughts flitted across her mind: thoughts of her mother, her brothers. I felt the tension build up in her body. The rhythmic pulsation of her blood sounded in my ears. The wide, swirling waters of the Limpopo stretched out before her. Though terrifying, the vision of the snake-like river sparked a light of hope. She knew what she had to do.

"Get out!" She turned to see a policeman standing on the bank behind her. She pushed on as fast as she could. The water weighed heavily against her legs. The sound of splashing water told her he was in after her. Alarmed, she struggled onwards. They were both hip-deep in water, and he was gaining on her. Spurred on by fear, she forced her way to the far bank.

Dripping, she collapsed with a low thud onto the mud of the riverbank. Her eyes blurred, moving in and out of vision like a malfunctioning screen. Again the pain throbbed in her abdomen and blackness drew down her eyes.

She awoke to a growing agony. As she opened her eyes, her face distorted in pain, she noticed a swarm of brown, faded uniforms surrounding her. The pain finally overcame the terror that grasped her heart. Short, dry gasps escaped her lips. A muffled sound reached me, the intermingled voices no longer individually discernable. The throbbing ache reverberated in her head. By now her moans were clearly audible. I stirred. Images rolled before her eyes: her family and her future. A sensation of warm wetness flooded her legs before blackness drew down again.

Her lids opened to daylight and more voices. Questioning murmurs and whispers of wonder. "We didn't think she could make it," the voice filtered into her consciousness. She lay amidst a circle of concerned faces and official badges. It was my turn to take a breath and let out a feeble warbling. She scanned her surroundings; a glittering border fence at dawn met her eyes. A smile lit up my mother's face. A river of tears began to wash down her cheeks as she welcomed me, her mewling baby, into her arms. I am born.

Nightmare Alive

Trevor Carlsson

To and fro, I watched the pendulum swing. The grandfather clock stood in the corner towering above everything else, and, still hypnotised by its steady movement, I felt time slow down. Perspiration trickled down my back as I listened intently to the thump of my heart in the silence; nothing else mattered any more. Closing my eyes I felt the air being drawn out of me...

Waking up drenched in cold sweat I gasped for air, and placed my right hand over my heart where I felt it pound. It was just a dream. Lifting myself slowly off my pillow, a sharp pain shot through my head and it began to throb almost instantly. "Just the way I wanted to start the day," I said to myself. Reaching for my radio I gave the small dial a half-turn to switch it on. Nothing happened. It lay dormant, just sitting there and serving no purpose. No electricity again; the day was getting worse by the minute. Crawling out of bed I placed my feet gently into my slippers and proceeded to get ready.

I lived in a densely populated area in an old fashioned house that stood out like a lion among a flock of sheep. The streets that ran through the area were always congested with cars and the pavements crowded with people bustling about. It was utter mayhem. Stepping out of my gate and into the outside world, I clutched the strap of my bag tightly to avoid it being snatched by a thief. To my disbelief, the roads and pathways were empty. Not even the birds that usually sang melodies that awakened the soul could be heard. Something was terribly wrong.

Running from house to house I banged on the doors of as many of the neighbours as I could. Nobody answered. Turning into the main road to the city I stopped dead in my tracks, the whole city seemed dead silent. I felt faint.

Moving towards the closest street lamp I wrapped my arms around its cold surface and closed my eyes. I tried so hard to make the empty feeling go away, but it was no use. It was not going away, not so long as confusion clouded my mind.

Pushing off from the lamppost I decided to head for a telephone booth. Frantically pushing the buttons I waited for a dial tone, but the phone was dead. Dropping the handset I took a few stumbling steps back and fell to my knees. Trembling, I hugged myself tight and tried to think. Reaching into my pocket for my cell phone I knew I was kidding myself, and I was right. No signal. Calming myself by playing my favourite track on my cell phone I picked myself up off the rough surface of the road.

As I walked through the city the feeling of being completely alone in the world intensified. All the shops were open and everything was as it should be, save for one detail – no people. Entering one of the shops I wondered what would happen if I walked out with some stuff? I knew that I had not totally grasped the gravity of the situation, but you must agree, it was just so tempting. I could not help myself. Conspicuously I strolled up to a shelf of biscuits and grabbed a pack before bolting out of the store. Nothing happened. No alarm went off. There was no one to do anything about it.

The entire day became one big looting spree. Everything I ever wanted I took. In spite of this, there was no joy, I was so lonely by the end of the day. I didn't care anymore about the things I had taken or the places I had been or even the freedom I had experienced. I returned home. In frustration and anger, I wrecked everything I could see until my hands hurt. Exhausted I fell onto the couch beside me and began to cry. What was happening to me? Where was everybody? There was no explanation.

Now early evening, I lit some candles and prepared for bed. Laying my still throbbing head on my pillow, I reassured myself that when I awoke I would find that it had all been a terrible dream. Closing my eyes I positioned my body as best I could for the comfortable sleep that would surely rid me of my misery. Pondering aimlessly I scouted all the facts that I could gather and tried to come to a rational conclusion, but nothing came of the effort.

Opening my eyes after what seemed like a long and deep slumber, I was surprised to find that it still looked dark outside. Looking up at the clock my eyes widened, I had not been asleep at all! It just could not be. Running to the kitchen to verify what I feared was true; the clock there read exactly what the one in my bedroom did. I sat down and threw one of my slippers at the clock in exasperation.

If I couldn't get to sleep I would browse through some family photographs, I thought to myself. Scurrying through the house in desperation, I searched high and low before finally coming across the album. Running my unsteady fingers over the brown leather cover that encased the faces of those that I held closest to my heart, a tear ran down my cheek. Opening the album my eyes searched the page for a familiar face. Turning the pages faster and faster, I could feel panic rising. I was the only one in the photographs, standing beside blurry shadows. Terrified at what I saw, I angrily threw the book across the room and ran outside. Screaming at the top of my voice, I ran through the streets until I was finally tired and lost.

Cold and afraid of what to expect next, I curled up into a small ball and wept. I felt so isolated, so unsure of reality, even unsure if I was hallucinating. Picking myself up off the road I walked into the night, planting my feet carefully one in front of the other as I moved through the darkness. It was a strange feeling like no other I had ever felt before, movement in dead silence in pitch darkness, not knowing where I was in the world. I hated it. Shivering, I clapped my hands together. The sound scared me so much that I actually jumped. Walking further on something unexpected happened; I heard a voice…

Clenching my teeth and making fists I crept towards the voice. The night seemingly grew colder with every step I took towards the mysterious voice, and, slowing my strides, I approached more cautiously. I could not make out the words but the voice had an overwhelming force of attraction, drawing me closer and closer to it. Suddenly I came upon a bright light that forced me to shut my eyes. On opening them I could not believe what I saw, I was back home once more! I was beyond puzzled.

By now I was extremely tired, and could not help but drop onto my bed. It felt like I had been walking all night. My eyes and my legs both ached, but I could not close my eyes. I tried, but it was no use. Looking up at the clock once again I began to laugh, not that anything was in the least bit funny, but that was all that came out of my mouth. Was I hallucinating? I didn't know. What I did know was that it was impossible that less than five minutes had passed since the time I left the house…

Lying there on the bed I thought to myself about the little things in life I had always taken for granted. My dog, which was nowhere to be seen, crossed my mind. I experienced flash backs of all the special moments in my life. In the morning I would give all those that I loved a great big hug. I took one last look up at the clock that seemed to be tormenting me, and concentrated on its shiny pendulum.

It moved to and fro in a hypnotising movement that seemed to slow time down. The temperature rose suddenly and the voice sounded once more as I felt myself sweating profusely. My heart thumped loudly before the voice ceased and everything went silent. Gradually, my eyes began to close and, feeling breathless, I blacked out.

On waking I breathed in deeply and instantly noticed the beautiful rays of sunlight that shone throughout the house. It was finally morning! Looking up at the clock to make sure I was not dreaming, I jumped for joy. The wait was over and I could continue life once more. Running outside with a smile from ear to ear, I froze…

The streets were empty, and the silence was even more oppressive. It could not be, but it was. Did the clock have something to do with it? It was starting all over again. My nightmare was alive…

So Sad The Song

Bongiwenkosi N. Zulu

So sad the song that is for me
A mask I hold to mercilessly
A joyous melodious symphony
That you might never ever see
The troubles that lay deep in me.

So sad the song that weaves for me
An everlasting reverie
That you might never reach my heart
My mind, my soul a land apart.

So sad the song that's shielding me
Forever hiding in secrecy
An ever-changing face of mystery
As fleeting as the morning dew.

Its ravenous flames lick hungrily at me
Spreads rapidly like a fire left to breathe
Slowly taking and making a life of its own
Like a tide drenching and wrenching my soul
Silently fear makes me its own.

So sad the song that is for me
A sacred flame to dark crevices leads
That guides my sad and lonely heart
That I may never receive again
The glorious light of day
A touch of love, an embrace
The distant dreams of yesterday.

So sad the song that is for me
As night Her cloak of ebony seeks,
Encompassing and engulfing me
Hence my sad song of misery
Forever remains a mystery
Forever hidden in secrecy.

Caine, My Friend, My Lover

Samantha Luiz

Grinning broadly, I closed my eyes, suddenly elated with the whole world and life itself. Feeling my soul happily glide from one cloud to another before peacefully resting on one marked 'nine', I sighed, happy and serene. That was the effect Caine had on me. Beloved Caine, my friend, my lover. I opened my eyes and gazed lovingly. Undoubtedly he was very different. He was special, I decided finally, after searching my limited vocabulary for a word that best described him. He had diverse qualities that people sought after, amongst them a mystical ability to make one forget all problems. Caine wasn't artificial, he was real, and did not go with the crowd. He had the ability to envelope me in a blanket of ecstasy, a high or a rush that made me sigh in enchantment. It was almost perfect. Almost... I was in love and viewed him as a manifestation of my dreams. Soon I grew an incessant need for him, and compared him to the air I breathed – the fatal need. If truth be told, I had fallen for him hook, line and sinker.

'Too much of a good thing is bad for a growing girl's health' sounds like a typical old wives' tale, but somehow I could relate to it, for too much of Caine was bad. I had grown an insatiable dependence on him and would have done anything for him, it was as if an invisible force was binding me. I hated how much I loved him, despised how much I adored him, but I just could not let him go... How could I, when he made my body think and feel a million different things? No doubt, I was at his mercy. But he was not perfect. The perks that accompanied my love came along with flaws. Those around me loathed, despised Caine, the entrapment into which he had led me, and the effect of loving somebody who pulled you down... Enough is enough, they decided, Caine had to go.

That was a year ago. I adjust my eyes to the depressingly foreign room. It is austere-looking, comprising a single bed and a vase of artificial daisies on a bedside table that do anything but brighten up the room. On the plainly painted, claustrophobic walls hangs a portrait of a Victorian woman wearing what looks to me like an artificial smile. Surrounded by the artificial, my memories are the closest thing to real I have. As this thought builds inside my head, a wave of nostalgia washes over me, enveloping me in a blanket of sentimental longing for the past. As suddenly as it appears, the feeling vanishes and I am returned to reality, a cold, harsh reality. I had been taken back to my friendship days with Caine. Even up to this day I still don't remember exactly how I came to allow Caine to have total control over me. Caine, who was my friend and first love.

A turn of the handle breaks my chain of thought as a pretty young woman carrying a tray with my lunch enters. She smiles. "Artificial," I think, suddenly craving for Caine. But sometimes when you love someone so much you have to let them go, surely?

I smile back at the nurse and begin picking at the food, brushing aside all thoughts of Caine. Glancing at the nurse before she closes the door behind her, I wonder whether she has ever had a friend like mine. Or not. I guess not. To many, Caine is an artificial being, a mere substance that had disastrous effects on me. He was addictive. Some called him cocaine, and others snow. To me, he was just Caine, my friend, my lover.

Briefly glancing at the claustrophobic walls of the Rehab Clinic, I sigh heavily. Deciding there and then it was unhealthy to have such a rigid dependence, I say to no-one in particular, "Goodbye, Caine."

The Face of Truth

Bongani Ncube

Chaos reigns on the streets of Algiers.

The city embraces the ocean in a warm hug, the buildings seeming to dare to meet the coastline and submerge themselves in its blue vastness. But as much as they dare, they stand just short of the beach, aloof and yet friendly, white slabs in the shimmering Mediterranean sun with their blue balconies and the array of satellite dishes on every available roof. The streets below speak of chaos. The toot of horns and the rumble of the voices of the crowds permeate the air of the Algiers streets like the heat that affects every living being beneath the burning sun. And yet life goes on as it always does regardless of the weather, people walk about everywhere conducting their business, half an eye on the heavens hoping for just one passing cloud to relieve them of the summer heat, the rest of their concentration on the business at hand, the business of living.

And everyone gets on with their lives. The smart young businessmen in their designer suits, ears attached to their cellphones, hands in their pockets, weaving through the crowds on the pavements. The shop owners who patiently sit on little chairs outside their shops waiting for customers to come in, their eyes scanning the crowd as if somehow they can pick up potential buyers with the power of their minds alone. The old men sitting at the tables outside the cafés, slowly sipping on their tumblers of thick black coffee, savouring the liquid that has stained their teeth yellow. The old women go about their business covered from tip to toe in black, only their eyes peering through the slits of their *hijabs* giving a hint of another world.

But any eye looking around would see more than a hint of tension between the old and the new. As a young girl walks by in a skirt cut above the knee, she passes a mother wearing an ankle length dress and a veil that covers the lower half of her face. Men, recently from the mosque, sitting at the café tables, wonder at the youths passing by on the street in clothes fashioned in France. Heads shake now and again as the thought runs through their minds that this world is not as it should be.

"*As-salāmu alaikum.*" One can hear the ancient Islamic greeting from one pair of friends as another pair exchange four kisses on the cheeks, French style. The modern and the old, perched uncomfortably on the same branch of a small tree, like two birds, aware that one must fly away or they will both fall, yet all they do is regard each other with half closed eyes and hardened hearts. But the eye, human as it is, can ignore such tension as exists on the streets of Algiers, preferring to settle on more pleasant matters.

Perhaps the smile of the child who sits at a restaurant table, with her mother, eating ice cream, her brown eyes beaming as she devours her favourite treat. Or the sight of the slowly rotating stacks of meat on the grills stationed on the pavements that will soon be used to make that uniquely Arab snack, the *shwarma*: flat bread loaded with meat and chips, eggs and lettuce then generously drizzled with mayonnaise and spicy sauce. Or maybe the laugh of the smart young woman, laden with groceries, in her designer suit, as she stands outside a boutique unloading some gossip on a friend she has encountered by happy chance on the doorstep. Perhaps even the tremulous smile of the young man who is walking to the base of the statue that stands at the centre of the square, a lion in the act of pouncing, its bronze muscles tensed in anticipation of the deathly leap that will never be.

But perhaps not the last one. His smile has vanished as if the lion has scared the joy out of him and, on looking at him more closely, one can see the grimace on his long thin face. His lips are moving rapidly and, listening carefully, one can hear words of hurt and anger. Even as the mind begins to try to comprehend the rapid outpouring of Arabic, one notices the nervous tic on his cheek and the bulky jacket he is wearing in this heat. But the words again grab the attention, words filled with hate for this world of corruption and sin, of institutionalised lust and corporate greed. There are prayers as well, of hope that action is the way of the blessed and inaction a sign of weakness, prayers to a God who seems to demand violence for the eternal peace of his soul. He looks about him and prays that he is doing the right thing.

But as always, human as it is, the eye looks for more pleasant things to settle upon. And it finds them. The little girl has spilt ice cream on her dress and for a moment the pout of her full lips seems to presage a stream of tears. Her mother leans forward in her chair, wipes the gob of ice cream off the front of her daughter's dress and laughingly offers her ice-cream covered finger for the girl to lick. Her eyes light up and she gives a giggle of pure joy, unburdened by any tension. The sound strikes through to the core of the heart, hardened as it might be, reminding all who hear it of the goodness that exists everywhere if only one looks hard enough.

And for a moment the young man is frozen in his tracks. His eyes meet those of the little girl across the chasm that separates them and in them he sees the beauty of God, the life that is the real business of this world. For a moment he sees Truth.

But only for a moment, because it is too late. Too late for him as the explosives wrapped around his chest detonate. Too late for the little girl as her ice cream is vaporised into nothingness. Too late for forty-three other people in that square on that summer day. But never too late for the truth. The young suicide bomber dies seeing something that, in his life, he had closed his eyes to. And perhaps there will be a price to pay on the other side? Who knows? Certainly not the people in the streets of Algiers as the bomb blast rips through the fabric of the city's life.

Yes, there is tension in the streets of the city, but the truth still remains.

Hell

Khayelihle Moyo

'Lord, please be with me. Deliver me, oh Lord!' I pray silently as I hurriedly step onto the train. The other passengers seem to stare at me curiously as I make my way to an empty seat. I seat myself timidly and tightly clutch against my chest my small bag containing a few belongings: a shirt, a pair of boxer shorts, a notepad, a pencil, a knife and a small amount of money. I hunch up as small as I can and pull down the visor of my cap. I cannot risk being seen, not that anyone on the train would recognise me. The fact that I am a schoolboy travelling in term time could lead to an interrogation, for which my fragile mind is not ready.

As I debate with myself whether to go home or not, my mind slowly drifts back to the place from which I am running. School. My mind sails through the warm summer night, past the stars and the bright crescent moon, to the very first day I stepped into the miserable place that became my worst nightmare. Literally, a living hell.

Clad in a blazer, a shirt with a striped tie, grey shorts, long socks and black shoes, I felt so proud. I had worked tirelessly to get into the very best high school; and my parents took pride in me, their only son, Lesley Vilakazi. I could see myself becoming a huge success in the world of corporate finance. My parents and I selected this high school because of its reputation and its excellent examination results. This single-sex school was quite a distance away from my home, roughly three hundred kilometres, so I was compelled to be a boarder. This did not worry me greatly as I felt I could fend for myself. What could possibly go wrong? If only I had known the horrors that awaited me behind the dormitory walls and doors.

My first week of school had been pleasant and I had quickly adapted to my new surroundings. I had written to my parents telling them about my first week at the school. Unfortunately, this was going to be my first and last honest letter home. The weeks that followed were to be horrific! The first time it happened I was left shell-shocked.

It was after supper on a Friday evening, and the multitudes rushed out of the Dining Hall, eager to get to their dormitories and kick-start the weekend. A senior had pulled me aside and told me to meet him in his room in thirty minutes. I, being a meek *mafikizolo*, unthinkingly obliged. At the appointed time, I rapped on the wooden door, and a deep voice from inside the room commanded me to enter. I slowly turned the handle and stepped inside, looking around the room as the door closed behind me. There they were, the 'Four Devils' that were to turn my life into a waking nightmare. The two on the top bunks climbed down and slowly advanced towards me.

They warned me to be quiet and that, if I made the slightest sound, or said anything to anyone later, they would kill me. These words terrified me, and added goose bumps upon goose bumps. I felt like screaming, but there was a huge lump in my throat. Breathing became difficult.

The two forced me to the floor and held me down. The other two stripped off my shorts and boxer shorts. Paralysed, I could do nothing as the devils took turns inflicting tremendous pain... raping me. They taunted and jeered at me, mocking my stupidity and my vulnerability. They continued this for what seemed like an interminable time, then finally let go of me. One of them reminded me of their threat and that, as seniors, they could get away with anything. I dared not say a word to anyone.

A nudge brings me back to the present. I turn to my left, where a young man of about twenty is looking at me suspiciously. I straighten my body position as he asks me what I am doing on the train. Words flood my mind as I search for the perfect lie. Finally, I blurt out the truth – that I am running away from school. My statement obviously shocks him, and he wants to know why I am running away from one of the best schools in the country. I curse myself for being stupid: You could have said you had been sent to your uncle by your mother! You fool! Who knows what this chap will decide to do?

There is no escaping my memories as my mind replays the many times I was abused. It became a weekly routine. Every Friday evening, after supper, I provided entertainment for the 'Four Devils'. I recall the malicious expressions on their faces as they tormented me. On one occasion, the devils invited their friends and dressed me as a girl, and I was forced to dance in front of them. Whenever I was abused by the devils the pain was always excruciating. Every Friday night I bled and I cried myself to sleep.

I often wondered if other juniors went through the same hell as I did. But I dared not ask. I knew that I should have informed the school authorities about these sexual offenders. But I was so scared of what the devils would do to me. I became reserved, drowning in my world of fear and my hate for the 'Four Devils'. My parents fretted over my deteriorating grades, but I couldn't even hint to them of the reason why my marks had dropped.

Here I am, slouched, in a train, running away. Running away from a living hell. Leaving the place that has left me with scars and bruises, both emotional and physical. My silence seems to disturb the young man. He continues to ask me questions, but gets no response. I can hear his words, but I cannot bring myself to answer. It is as if I have been struck dumb. Before the young man can get any answers from me, the train stops; he has reached his destination. He murmurs a few words, looks worried, and leaves.

Five minutes later, we are on the move again. I listen intently to the chugging of the train. My running away has become a contentious issue between two voices in my mind. One is telling me to head home and disclose the full story to my parents. The other tells me to just end my miserable life. I had dreams and goals to fulfil, but my tormentors have made me forget my aspirations. Due to their actions, I feel worthless. I succumbed to them, bowed down to them.

Tears fall from my eyes. They roll down my cheeks and die at my lips. How I had wished for someone to comfort me and help me overcome these troubles. But it is too late. I dig my hands inside my bag. I pull out my pencil, knife and notebook. I start to write a note. Firstly, I write my address and telephone number. On the second page I write a letter to my parents. I thank them for all they have done for me. I write down the details of my ordeal. I sign, and close the notebook. I let out a loud maniacal laugh. I will die at ease, knowing that the 'Four Devils' will be there to meet me, in Hell! Yes, I murdered them! All that remains for me now is to end my life, and I pick up the knife.

Disabled

Basil Dube

Being disabled does not mean
I am not a human being.
I might be blind,
I might not walk,
I might not talk,
But I am a human being just like you.

I have blood,
I have teeth,
I breathe,
Just like you.
But you say I am disabled.

I can work,
I can eat,
I can learn,
Just like you.
But you say I am disabled.

God created us to love each other,
Not to laugh at each other.
I am a human being just like you.

The Colour Line

Nqobizitha Malusi Nkomo

"I love you," whispered Laura. Three simple words, but the smile on my face dissolved as I thought of the path the words might take us down.

"Laura, you know I love you, but…"

"No buts, Mark. We can work things out," Laura interjected.

"I was thinking more of your parents…"

"What about them?" Laura burst in again. "It's you I'm in love with so what are you worried about?"

"It's just that… I'm black and eh… eh… you are white," I stammered.

"Well we'll just have to convince my parents that it's you I love, won't we?" Laura said smugly.

I walked home with my head abuzz. How would I tell my parents I would be bringing a white girl home? How would Laura's parents react to our relationship? All these questions so distracted me that when I looked around I realised that I had walked right past my home. Reluctantly I turned around and, like a prisoner approaching the dock, I entered our house.

"What!" my father spluttered, my mother's eyes bulged as she looked heavenward as if seeking divine intervention and my brother choked on his food. All this I took in before the storm broke.

"Mark, are you crazy? Do you want to bring shame to the family name? Mama, is this what you teach your son to do?" Father erupted.

"What? Is this not your son too? Don't blame me for his folly." Mother snapped back.

"Mark, answer me this question. Who are you? Do you think that this white girl of yours will bear you fine strong sons? Do you think she will love you forever? Answer me!" Father thundered.

"Well…" I began but didn't get far before Mother voiced her anger too.

"Mark, how can you shame me so much, eh? What will my friends think when they find out my daughter-in-law is white?"

"But, Mother…" Once again I didn't finish.

"No buts, boy! No son of mine will marry a white girl, you hear? And you are banned from seeing her ever again. There are some very decent black girls in the neighbourhood so bring one of them home and we will continue this discussion further. Till then, discussion closed." Father banged his fist on the table, upsetting the soup bowl.

Who am I? This question hovered over me like a hungry mosquito seeking blood. I tried to sleep, but it merely landed on me, crushing me to the bed, suffocating me. Who are you? the walls seemed to echo till the room vibrated. I thought I was going crazy when Laura suddenly appeared in front of my bed, her face puzzled, questioning: "Mark, who are you?" As I opened my mouth to speak, Laura's face dissolved and took the form of my father's, then of my mother's; all questioning me, "Mark, who are you?"

Then Laura's body disintegrated before my eyes and turned into a creature with wings but without a face, calling in a shrill voice, "Mark, Mark, who are you?" I put my head under the pillow to hide from the cacophony of voices.

After a couple of days things quietened down at home. Mom stopped shouting and calling me a "senseless boy with no identity" and Father stopped muttering "crazy fool" every time I passed within his vicinity. Of Laura there was no word, and I assumed that her parents had given her a verbal thrashing and probably banned her from setting her pretty eyes on me ever again. Perhaps the time had come for me to get back to my roots, but I could not banish the image of Laura from my mind.

On the next Saturday morning, when I woke up, there was a white dove sitting on my window ledge and, while I was staring at it, a crow came and perched next to the dove and the two birds flew away together. Around two o'clock that afternoon there was a knock on the front door, and my young brother answered it.

"Is Mark in?" a familiar voice asked.

"I don't think he's supposed to see you," my brother responded curtly.

"Well I'm here now and really need to see him," the voice said defiantly.

I ran from my room at the back of the house towards the front door. "Laura!" I joyously cried and would have run to hug her if my father had not come out of the living room in front of me.

"So you are the Laura who has led my son astray," Father said.

"I am Laura, sir," Laura announced. "And I've come to see Mark."

"My son does not want to see you," my father began. "There can be no relationship between a son of mine and a white girl. And I'm sure your family feel exactly the same way." He turned around to the man and woman who came to stand behind Laura.

He continued in the same vein, "For what friendship can black have with white?"

"This is getting us nowhere," Laura's father said from the doorway.

Laura joined in, "Please, can we not talk about this."

"The girl is right," my mother responded, and invited Laura and her parents into the living room. "I will make some tea for us all."

A long conversation ensued between the families. Both sets of parents strongly expressed their opinion that only difficulties would lay ahead for a couple who chose to cross the racial barrier in the union of marriage.

Laura then interjected, "But I love Mark. We know it won't be easy."

Laura's belief in our relationship gave me the courage to speak up.

"Father, I remember when you asked me who I was. Well, I am now ready to answer you."

I dared not look at my father's face. "I asked myself what identity meant. It means that I am human, regardless of my skin colour. I am proud of my ancestry, but it should not affect my choice of partner. It does not matter to me that Laura is a different colour to me. I love Laura and I can't see a future without her." I ended as Laura came and sat next to me.

It took all my strength to stand up to my father, his word had always been law in our home, and I was nervous as to how he would respond.

My father started to speak, "Well son, I still have grave reservations about this matter. But, if Laura's parents agree, let's see how the relationship works out over the next few months."

"That seems reasonable," Laura's father responded. "That would give us the chance to get to know Mark and for you to get to know Laura."

My father said, "I am sorry for my earlier behaviour. We were just so concerned for our son as I'm sure you were for Laura. I think the strength of their feelings for each other has been demonstrated today. Our role as parents should now be to support them as much as we can."

I hugged Laura as our parents looked on and started to think that a future with Laura might be possible after all.

Life in the Ghetto

Siphosethu Mpofu

The winds of time blow away everything in their path, leaving only faint traces of what occurred in the distant past, but no winds can ever completely blow away the good old days with memories of fame, glory and the fall of giants. This is my story, a story that has no end, no final episode, like a magnet it brings together the past and the present, creating an inevitable future. It begins in the backyard of high buildings, well away from gracious mansions, flashy cars and the fancy life. It's the story of where I was born and bred, where I belong – the ghetto.

It was never a safe place for everyone. You had to know the surroundings in and out. The right shortcut to your destination, the right time to think about a visit to the toilet. We were so frightened of the horrors of the night that we preferred to use buckets as toilets rather than allow the horror to devour us. I recall one night awakening to the shrill screams of a woman, whom I later learnt had been stabbed, robbed and left for dead. Any attempts at rescue would have been foolhardy as you would seriously risk losing your own life in the process.

Such crimes were so prevalent that we barely trusted one another; we never left clothes hanging on the fence unattended or did business transactions with a total stranger. Before we slept we thoroughly checked all the doors, the windows and the gates to establish that they were well secured. Of course we never had sliding gates, so our small wooden gate was tightened with wires so that it would have taken a knot maestro to untangle them and, by then, we would have been wide awake and ready for battle. It was the survival of the bravest and better skilled.

Fancy a Saturday morning stroll? The scandalous *omatshaya inyoka* of the ghetto were a common sight on street corners. Some debated controversial football issues, some shared a jug of opaque beer, while others quarrelled about one thing or another. They all had one thing in common, begging, from a cent, a dollar, to a thousand, for another round of opaque beer. Once upon a time, they were 'to be' giants and the world revolved around them. They had passions, some had dreams and hopes, whilst others had ways and means, to be motor mechanics, footballers, or economic analysts, but most are now fading pictures, broken images and incomplete stories of what could have been.

As I grew up I got used to this life, a life full of misery and pain. Imagine the unfairness of life – one could see a hobo dying of hunger and cold while the filthy rich *ingagara* of our hood were feeding their dogs with drumstick left overs and allowing them to sleep on comfortable, though overused, rugs.

Nonetheless, *enkomponi*, as it was affectionately known, had its lighter moments. It came to life at weekends. I remember the glory of Happy Valley Tavern, the live bands, the discos, not forgetting the fame it had for charging exorbitantly for its services. I recall the persuasive power shebeens had on men with 'talking wallets', with omaMoyo, oJane and oSandra offering everything in one package.

To ease the hangover on Sunday, or just thirst for a blessing, church was the answer. This is where anybody met everybody. The pastor would shower the congregation with heavenly praises coupled with words of prayerful joy. Suddenly everyone would just crumble like a deck of cards: the thieves, the soldiers, the soccer fans, the drunkards, you name them, all would join in – leaping from their seats and rolling in the aisles. The celebration was reminiscent of the glitz and glamour that Barbourfields Stadium carried on its shoulders; the players, the goals, the dramatic moments and the faces that forgot they were mothers, fathers, pastors or police as they cheered on their favourite teams.

My home, the ghetto, the memory is as vivid as the blue sky above. Visit the ghetto today and the same winds still blow. Winds that witness the disparate elements and people that make up the jigsaw that is life in the ghetto. My ghetto.

Life of a Zimbabwean

Michael Hove

This is a story about the life of a Zimbabwean. It is my story, your story, our story. It is not an easy story to tell.

I start work at six o'clock, but in order to get there in time I have to wake up as early as four o'clock. My aim is to catch the commuter train that departs at a quarter to five at the sub-station. In the space of forty-five minutes I manage to take a bath and dive into my oily overalls. Quickly I eat last night's leftovers. Before I leave you might expect me to brush my teeth, but no, I consider buying toothpaste a luxury. That's not my lifestyle. I know I have enough time to make it to the station but I don't have time to kiss my wife goodbye, instead I leave her covered in a cold blanket of love.

When I leave the house the first thing that my filthy breath stabs is the cold dark air. Life seems too cold. When I arrive at the station the ticket issuer, 'Black Jack', chats with me as we wait for the train to depart. "Ahh Mandla, how are you this early morning? You know I heard that the commuter bus fares were raised last night. All the *salalas* will come flocking here to disturb our peace."

"Then there's going to be a battle of odours, for us the loyal children of the train shall respond with our armpit power to their artificial perfumes."

'Black Jack' laughs at my response. The loud train horn alerts everyone that the time has come to take those who want to live the next day to work. As we journey on, listening to the talk of other passengers, mostly men, makes the hour long journey seem short. The main topic of discussion is the country's unstable economy. One of the men involved in the discussion looks at me with a stern eye that invites me to comment, but no, I prefer to observe silence.

Their talk drifts from politics to sport, particularly soccer. Some express their pain that a popular local football club has transferred one of its youngest and most talented players across the border to a bigger club. Most fear that without the player's skill the club may not be able to claim the premiership league title. But others think that it is good for the country's interests to expose the player to the much more competitive league. Again, silence best suits me.

When the train hits *burg*, the main station becomes a hive of activity as everyone rushes to their workplace. In thirty minutes I manage to cover the hour long journey to work on foot. Being short, it's hard work covering so much ground so fast, but far easier than explaining a late arrival to the angry fat foreman. In my own house I'm the boss. No one orders me what to do there. My wife and child might not like it, but it feels good to me. But my dominion is short-lived when I arrive in work. Here, I'm as an ant on a bear's foot. I can't even complain to my employer about the ill treatment from the foreman. To complain would be a ticket to being jobless. There is no freedom of speech here. "Ahh my friend you are lying. Freedom of speech is there, but there is no freedom after the speech," my workmate laughs.

The work is oppressive and alienating. I work hard for twelve hours a day, but the rewards are so disheartening. I'm merely 'a cog in the wheel'.

But it is hard to speak out in this long existing passive culture of silence. I'm not too sure whether it's fear or just apathy. I remember last week being so happy that I decided to splash out by catching a commuter omnibus home from work. Like all the other passengers, I had twenty billion dollars ready to pay the correct fare, but the conductor insisted we top up with another twenty billion. He had raised the fares. No one complained except for one old drunk man clinging loosely to his consciousness. But the young dread-locked *windie* was quick to threaten the old man with dropping him off before his desired destination if he failed to pay the 'full' fare.

The young man's voice echoed right into our semi-empty pockets and meekly we topped up the fare. I couldn't believe it. Of the twenty passengers, only one drunken man managed to speak out. Although he eventually topped up the fare, he continued to complain and to insult the *windie*. "*Wena mfana, wena*. I'm so much better than you. I went to school and passed and I'm drinking my own money that I worked for. Unlike you who I bet does not even know whether he's left or right handed simply because you have never been to school and you don't know which hand you use for writing."

But the young man couldn't care less about the insults. He had been paid. Instead his eyes rested on the old man's bottle. He was capable of reading the eight letter word, *Mainstay*, perhaps imagining the colourless liquid quenching his thirst. But his desires were not to be met that evening, instead he nonchalantly chewed on a matchstick, occasionally flipping it from one side of his mouth to the other.

Well that is how life has always been. 'Thou shalt not speak'. Voiceless, I continue with my work, playing the oppressed. Once again, I feel that life is just too cold, it is better to be dead. Dead people don't go hungry; they just lie down there, resting, dead. You know, one day I almost got struck by a car and I wish it had killed me. I remember coming from the passport office where I'd just been given bad news. I'd just been informed that the passport I had applied for two years previously had still not been processed.

Silently, sadly, I walked away from the information desk as the passport officer repeated, "next... next..." So, walking down the road, I almost got struck by a car that was being driven recklessly. "Hey, *wena*, watch where you are going. *Uyahlanya kanti?*" the driver shouted as he disappeared down the road with his van. These crazy drivers, famously known as *omalayitsha*. Whenever you see them, the weight of the goods they carry is twice that of their die-hard vehicles. My hope was lost. My hope of travelling abroad in search of greener pastures was lost once again. It is every Zimbabweans' dream to live in the diaspora. It doesn't matter how one lives there. All that matters is to come back home one day driving a sleek car bearing foreign number plates, to show off to your neighbours as your children struggle to offload the heavy groceries from the trailer of your car, to live that lavish life and forget about what the day after tomorrow has in store for you. But then, if everyone goes out there, who is going to stay behind?

As soon as the hour and minute hand both point at six on the factory clock that hangs on the oily wall for everyone to see, only the newly employed workers have a hard time remembering that it is time to knock off. For those of us who cannot cycle or walk home, it's time for the freedom train – the brown dash, *izinyoka* or the limousine. When I get to the station I quickly board the train, which is just about to leave. Inside the heat is intense. Old men and women, school children, the working generation, market women with live hens, boxes filled with tomatoes, onions, guavas and oranges fill up the train and create an overwhelming smell. Hunger, to which I am not a stranger, overcomes me. Samandlo, a vendor who has made a name for himself on the train for his kindness, sells me three sweets on credit. "I'll pay tomorrow Samandlo, *ungabi le pressure*," I lie to him. I abuse his kindness. Tomorrow he will not see me. I'll board the baggage coach; he never sells there. But for now his sweets cut the long journey short. After an hour the train arrives at the sub-station. The moment I drop off, I dream of a mountain of *sadza*, with a relish of fresh vegetables and heaps of meat.

When I get home, the first thing that greets me is the brown soup-stained two plate stove. It is cold. I question my wife, who responds, "Do you want me to cook water for you SaPrince, yeh! Do you?" She reminds me that it is that time of the month when you open the refrigerator to find that there is nothing in it except water containers. The empty fridge means that I will have to pay my neighbour a visit. My rich neighbour. He has a stunning four-bedroomed house that is durawalled. The satellite dish adds to the beauty of the house. It is a sign that he will have a kitchen packed with food. Only the really fortunate can buy bread and meat every day and such is my neighbour SaTendai. Before I call him, I take a peep over his durawall and see his latest car, a *Mazda 3*. He's already home.

I decide to ask SaTendai for some mealie meal. Just enough to make *sadza* for tonight. In asking for a favour, I need first to engage him in friendly conversation. I ask him about tonight's *Oprah Winfrey Show*. Wrong move. He starts to recount the whole show as hunger caresses my stomach. He talks and talks, thinking that I'm really interested.

By the time I am ready to ask the favour, SaTendai rushes into his house shouting, "I'll see you tomorrow my friend, my favourite comedy is about to start." He leaves me in the dark holding my empty yellow container, hoping for a miracle. The Son of God performed a miracle when he fed the five thousand and all that I'm asking for is to feed three people.

I slowly walk into my house. At least I have a roof over my head. This two-roomed house of mine serves as kitchen, dining-room, lounge and bedroom. For this I force a faint smile. I lie on the couch; tonight I cannot share a bed with my wife, who will be angry because I'm the reason why we will sleep on an empty stomach again. As I stare at the roof I count ten holes that allow the moon's light to cut through. The same holes let in the rain during the rainy season.

I think of my son. He's in grade three and is good at mathematics and English. My father gave me a chance to be educated and I blew it, hanging

103

out late at night, drinking and smoking. Perhaps there is a better future for my son. But for now, reality intrudes. Tonight I have to sleep on an empty stomach. Don't worry, I'm used to it, but when it happens to you, will you be ready for it? I don't know. I close my eyes and slowly drift into deep sleep.

Contributors

Trevor Carlsson (*Nightmare Alive*) is seventeen years old and is studying sciences in the upper sixth form at Masiyephambili College where he is Senior Prefect. His hobbies are cycling and writing as well as reading – his favourite book is *Lord Of The Rings*. He came first in the 2007 *Standard* short story competition in the form four category.

Sonia Chidakwa (*When You Look At Me*) is 22 years old and enjoys listening to music, socialising, reading and creative writing. Three of her poems were published in the anthology *Stars in a Plate*. She writes her poems from the heart.

Basil Dube (*Disabled*), aged 12, is in Form One at Foundation College. He likes reading, writing, playing cricket and going to school. His favourite food is rice and chicken.

Mercy T. Dube (*The Death of My Father*) is a form four student at Amhlophe Secondary School. In Mercy's words, born poor but rich in mind, she is ready and inspired to assert herself as one of the leading women voices in Zimbabwean poetry. She draws her inspiration from nature.

Rebecca Dube (*If Only*), aged 18, is in the Upper Sixth at Mzilikazi High School. She plays netball and is a member of Interact.

Brian Dzapasi (*Between the Lines*) is a National University of Science and Technology student of Banking. He says that ever since he held the pen, his life has never been the same. Through the pen, he expresses himself in poetic form, his deep seated passion.

Gamila Elmaadawy (*Borderline Birth*) is an 18 year old ex-Girls College student who loves music. She plays the guitar and plays in jazz bands. She wants to become a lawyer or a journalist.

Farai Godobo (*Uncle Tom Died*), aged 18, is an 'A' level student at Gloag High School He likes to read novels and writing poetry and prose. He can also act. He is inspired by Victor Thope.

Nadia Gori (*Racial Harmony*) is a 16 year old former EATC and Africombs student. Besides writing, her other passions are modelling and dancing.

Alfonce Munyaradzi Gova (*Identity and Diversity*) is a Refrigeration and Air Conditioning student at Zimbabwe College and is a youth leader at a local church. He is working on a novel that he hopes will be published in the near future. Besides writing, he is also interested in film and music.

Sarhanna Hassim (*My Sisters' Clothes*) is an upper sixth student at Girls College who enjoys writing about controversial issues. She is active member of a number of societies at her school, including Debate, Interact, Speakers Circle,and History, as well as being a member of Amnesty International.

Lee Hlalo (*The Tale of an African Forest*) is a 16 year old Form Four student at Girls College. She loves reading, and she loves pink. She enjoys Business Studies, doesn't do debate, but is very argumentative.

Michael Hove (*On the Streets*, *Life of a Zimbabwean* and *Mental Footpaths*), aged 22, finished his 'A' level studies at Princetop College in 2006. He runs an arts group for primary school children called Matabele Spirits Performing Arts Group. He loves reading and playing cricket in the Bulawayo Metropolitan League. His writing inspiration is Chenjerai Hove's *Ancestors*.

Tanya Hunt (*Being Different*) is a Lower Sixth student at Girls College. Tanya won the Intwasa Arts Festival koBulawayo youth short story competition in 2006. She loves horse riding and writing.

Thando Khuphe (*Skin*), aged 18, is currently pursuing his Advanced Levels at EATC College. He loves reading and writing short stories and would one day love to work in a newsroom.

Samantha Luiz (*Caine, My Friend, My Lover*), aged 17, is a former student at St. Gabriel's High School. Her literary achievements to date include first prize in the 2006 Cover to Cover short story competition and second prize in the 2008 Radio Dialogue sponsored *Through the Radio* short story competition.

Lindah Mafu (*The Token Woman*) is a 17 year old former Inyanda Secondary School student. Like all good writers, she is a enthusiastic reader. Her short story, Arena, was one of the winners of the Intwasa Arts Festival koBulawayo youth short story writing competition in 2006.

Khumbulani Malinga (*Bones*) is a 19 year old Nkulumane High School upper sixth student. An aspiring journalist and politician, he wants to use his writing skills to positively influence events in society.

Nobuhle Maposa (*If Only I Could Tell You*) is a student at Petra High School. She loves listening to music, dancing and socialising with friends.

Babongeni Zangelo Mlilo (*Jabu's Journey*), born in 1994, enjoys both academic study and sports. Zangelo has won several writing awards, including a prize for a competition run by The National Institute of Allied Arts in 2006 and a literary award for a competition run by Girl's College in the same year.

Bubelo Thabela Mlilo (*My Tribe*), born in 1996, has won numerous writing accolades at her primary school, Centenary. Her other writing achievements include a poetry prize for a competition run by The National Institute of Allied Arts in 2006 and a literary award for a competition run by Girl's College when she was 9 years old.

Gilmore T. Moyo (Cover art: *Silent Cry*) is a nineteen year old ex-student of St Gabriel's High School. As well as art, he is also interested in writing and was a finalist in the 2008 Umthwakazi Arts Festival short story competition.

Khayelihle Moyo (*Hell*) is 16 years old and passionate about drama and debate. She aspires to merge her love for psychology and music through her insightful rap...

Siphosethu Mpofu (*Life in the Ghetto*), aged 18, is studying history, literature and sociology at Zimbabwe College. He is an aspiring poet and actor, and is planning to study journalism and mass communications. This is his first short story.

Bongani Ncube (*Just Trust Me*, *Freedom* and *The Face of Truth*) is a 20 year old university student in Algeria. He was Zimbabwe National Debate Champion in 2005-6 and was a finalist in the Intwasa National Short Story Competition in 2007.

Nqobizitha Nkomo (*The Colour Line*) is a 21 year old UNISA Accounting Science student. His literary achievements to date include winning Girls College Literary Competitions and first prize in the 2004 National Youth Development Trust Essay Competition. His ambition is to write a novel that will change lives.

Zisunko Ndlovu (*Look At Me*) is a 19 year old writer, book reviewer and hip hop fanatic who hails from Binga. He is proud to be a product of Mpopoma High School.

Butholezwe K. Nyathi (Project Coordinator) is a holder of a BSc Honours Degree in Library and Information Science obtained from the National University of Science and Technology. Aged 23, he has a passion for youth development and sees the arts as a fun and interactive tool for streamlining young people's voices.

Babusi Nyoni (*Sistas* and *Heartbeats*) is aged 20. His passions are poetry, music, art and life. He aspires to be a graphic designer.

Lesley Phiri (*R. I. P.*) is an 18 year old upper sixth student at Nkulumane High School, who is affectionately known as Pastor Lesley. An award winning public speaker, Phiri is an aspiring lawyer and pastor.

Leanne Quindu (*If a Dog was the Teacher*) is a fifteen year old and a student at Petra High School. She was born in Botswana in a small town called Twaneng. Since the town was small and there was not much to do, she took up writing. She began writing in her diary then ventured into fiction. To her writing is a way of getting problems out of her system.

Faith Tshuma (*Wasted Years*) is an 18 year old who has finished her 'A' level studies at Pumula High School. Faith is passionate about writing and came second in the Intwasa Youth Short Story Competition. She is planning to study political science.

Novuyo Rosa Tshuma (*Scattered Hearts*, *The Beggar*, *The Controller of the Queue* and *Tears*) is in her first year at university. A novice writer of lofty literary ambitions, she won third prize in the Intwasa Short Story Competition 2008.

Bongiwenkosini N. Zulu *(So Sad The Song)*, aged 17, aspires to be a corporate lawyer, but prides herself on her writing skills that have resulted in publication in Cover to Cover and in this collection. She enjoys listening to music and drawing.

Thembelihle Zulu (*What You Did Not Read in the Headline*) aged 20, is an artist, dancer and songwriter who enjoys writing best of all. She hopes to become a marketing director.